The Great Deception:

Why Are They Here?

By: Stanley Simmons

Table of Contents

The Great Deception: Why Are They Here?

Published by VIP Ink Publishing

www.vipinkpublishing.com

Cover Art and Editing By Whyte Lady Designs
L.L.C.

ISBN 13: 978-0-9847382-7-4

ISBN: 0-9847382-7-4

Printed in the USA.

Chapter 1

Angels, Demons & UFOs - An Overview

I remember those warm summer nights when, even as a child, I would lie in the grass and gaze with wonder at the stars and speculate, who was out there and where did I fit into the scheme of things? Those two questions are still enigmas, but now more than ever, I think we need answers.

UFOs are nothing new. They have been here since dawn of time. With all the worlds in the vast universe, it seems our Earth and the races of man are not just curiosities, but obsessions with whoever occupies these unidentified flying objects.

As a Christian layman, I must take God at His Word. He never mentions UFOs as such but refers to observers, or to the Earth and man, as being a spectacle and that after a period of judgment, redeemed mankind and the angels who have remained faithful will rule the Earth and the universe as joint heirs with Christ. If one would ponder on the enormity of this promise to those who put their trust in Him until the reality of what it says becomes clear to one's mind and spirit, the implications become apparent.

Most people have come to accept UFOs as a reality. They have been seen by so many & are so well documented by reliable witnesses from all walks of life that denials by the military & the government are falling on deaf ears, & these military & government officials are losing their credibility with the general public.

1

I feel what science has discovered in the past one hundred or so years is but the tip of the iceberg. Our table of elements is hopelessly inadequate and laws of physics only cover but a tiny fraction of 'what is'. For every law there is another law to overcome it. The law of gravity can be overcome by the law of lift, and these UFOs have come up with several more laws to not just overcome gravity, but use it to their advantage.

What we have relegated to the paranormal and ESP are but extensions of scientific principles other races from the 'far countries' of the vast universe have probably been using for countless years. There is no reason for us to feel inadequate. After all, we have only been here for about six thousand years. We are just barely getting started.

The Scriptures refer to a race that was here before man. They were ruled by Lucifer, until he became so wicked that God had to destroy him and the creation that existed along with him. There is no record of how long that civilization was here or of how long the Earth remained 'without form and void' after that first destruction and first flood. Perhaps that older civilization was contemporary with some of our visitors in their UFOs.

For years I have waited, as I read book after book on the subject of flying saucers, for the church to say something to make sense of it all. I am still waiting. Perhaps the subject is too controversial or too much of a hot potato for anyone to speak out on. I am just a Christian layman who reads and studies the Bible and believes God has the answer for everything. I rely entirely on what God's Word says on the subject.

The existence of UFOs puts a damper on many heretofore comfortable beliefs of the scientific community and the religious community. It puts an enormous responsibility on the governments and the military of the different parts of the world which are expected to see to the security of their people.

I am firm in my belief that government cover-ups are but futile attempts to cover up what they do not know. If the general population of the Earth were to realize how inadequate our present governments and military are in the face of what these so called 'visitors' know, their ability to control us would be seriously threatened.

The purpose of international security is to maintain a workable stability among the nations of the world and for them, in turn, to retain institutional control over their respective populations. For these governments to admit that there are beings from outer space with mentalities and technological capabilities obviously far superior to ours would be devastating. Once the reality was fully perceived by the average person it would erode the foundations of earth's power structures.

The political and legal systems, religious, economic, and social institutions could all soon become meaningless in the minds of the people. This probably accurately reflects the fears of the ruling classes of the major nations, whose leaders have always advocated excessive government secrecy as necessary to preserve national security.

In 1972 scientist Werner Von Braun said, *"We cannot take credit for our record advancement in certain fields along; we have been helped by people of other worlds."*

There are persistent rumors that the United States has even test flown a few advanced vehicles, based on information allegedly acquired as a result of contact with extraterrestrials and the study of grounded UFOs.

In the November 1994 issue of the magazine, "New Mexico," is the story of the July 1947, crash at Roswell, New Mexico, of a flying disk and recovered alien bodies. In fact, there is a museum in Roswell that opened in 1992 that has this incident and others as their main theme. This Roswell crash is the subject of several books written by scientists, retired military officers, and laymen whose names and publications are listed in the bibliography.

Around the same time, there was another reported crashed saucer with alien remains retrieved on the plains of San Agustin, which is near the small town of Magdalena in New Mexico. The plains of San Agustin are now the location of the Very Large Array radio telescope. This second crash is only conjecture and has never been verified. Almost every book written on the UFOs mentions the crash at Roswell. That there has been other crashes since then is rumored, but the government has been quick and efficient in covering up all traces of such happenings.

If these 'people' from the far corners of the universe can crash, burn and die, this takes them out of the realm of angels, demons and devils. They are not supernatural! They are not gods! They are 'something' with an agenda of their own. What some of these agendas are should become apparent by the time you finish reading this book.

Men and women of impeccable reputation in fields of science, government, and the military have done painstaking and extensive research on these subjects. Including the existence of UFOs, their occupants, their relationship with man, and the abduction of many humans throughout the past forty or more years.

I have no intention of arguing the point with any of these people. My purpose in writing this book is to present the real reason why these visitors from other worlds and perhaps even from our own distant past or the nether regions of our own planet are here. Where do angels, demons, and devils fit into the puzzle?

After many years of painstaking research of my own, I believe I have found pieces to the puzzle that fit together to make a picture that will be believable to you. I do not write on this subject lightly. For those with impeccable reputations, it can be most damaging, which is why they back up what they say with such careful research, producing overwhelming evidence in favor of their subject, so much so that any court would have to find in their favor based on the given evidence.

UFOlogy has its' fringe group of frauds and hoaxers, who have obscured the truth, sadly enough, but truth cannot be hidden indefinitely. It only makes those determined to present the truth work harder to research and present their evidence of such happenings.

Religion also has its' share of frauds and hoaxers, making it more difficult for the true men and women of God to present what God has to say on the subject. Nevertheless, the church can no longer get away with remaining silent.

I have spent a vast amount of time researching whatever seemed a likely piece of the completed puzzle. In this book I am putting together all the puzzle pieces I have found. When the picture is completed, we will not only have a more clear idea of the agenda of our uninvited visitors, but of what God's plan for man really is.

What God has in store for man is so far reaching and mind boggling, it is no wonder others are here to observe it, to stop it, or to confuse it in any way that they can but, before we can understand our destiny, we must understand our origins, *"in the beginning!"* We the people need to be enlightened.

Thomas Jefferson (1748-1826) third president of the United States and principal author of the Declaration of Independence, in a letter to Charles Jarvis, September 28, 1820, said this:

"I know no safe depository of the ultimate powers of the society but the people themselves, and if we think them not enlightened enough to exercise control with a wholesome discretion,

the remedy is not to take it from them, but to inform their discretion."

President Ronald Reagan, in a speech in May of 1988, said, *"I've often wondered what if all of us discovered we were threatened by a power from outer space?"*

What indeed?

Chapter 2:

Origins

To fully appreciate our own existence we must also get some concept of the existence and later destruction of the creation that was here before us.

That inhabited worlds of that time were ruled by the powerful beings we call angels is evident by the fact that an angel called Lucifer, ruled the Earth before the creation of man (Ezekiel 28: 11-17). Here we have a picture of Lucifer before he fell, as the anointed cherub or protector of the Earth, being full of wisdom, perfect in beauty, and ruling from an Eden like garden. He was a being created by God, who was perfect in his ways up to the time iniquity was found in him.

There is no record of how much time elapsed from when he ruled in peace to the time iniquity was found in him and from then to the destruction of the Earth, and its inhabitants, who in choosing to follow, Lucifer shared in his punishment.

In view of how God has dealt with man throughout the ages according to Biblical and historical records, He must have given the people of this first creation, chance after chance to repent and change their ways before that final destruction. Perhaps the creation of those great beasts we know as dinosaurs was one of God's warning judgments against them. They would have had to be very resourceful just to survive in a world with such beasts. God created a whole new set of animals when He created man. This is evidence of God's mercy toward man right from the beginning.

Since Lucifer was full of wisdom, he had knowledge of forces we are only beginning to even be aware of. Let us suppose he taught the people who lived here then how to harness the elements, build space ships, and conquer space. Lucifer led one-third of the rest of God's angels to rebel against God as well as the races of the Earth. It only makes sense to conclude that these other angels also ruled planetary systems, which would have spread this 'rebellion' over vast distances and over populations of other worlds.

According to Isaiah 14:12-14, Lucifer actually invaded Heaven from the Earth, hoping to defeat God and take His kingdom, but Lucifer, himself, was defeated and his kingdom cursed.

How long would it have taken Lucifer to build up such an invasion force that he would feel confident that he could defeat God? Lucifer was and is an eternal being. He had all the time he needed to do the job right. In order to ever contemplate such a venture he would have had to teach the civilization over which he ruled the very secrets of the universe in order to have ships, weapons, and 'technological' abilities to carry out his plans. Other angels were helping him since he led one third of them.

Whether these angels involved any of their own civilizations with token forces of their own is a matter of conjecture. It is possible that many of our present visitors are descendants of those people. If this is so, it would be good

9

to keep in mind the evil intent that originated their interest in this planet and the one who ruled it in the first place.

The interplanetary invasion force must have been vast beyond anything we can imagine. Having weakened the nations over whom he ruled; weakness in this instance was the draining their spiritual values. He was determined to be like God and take God's place in Heaven and the universe. Lucifer led the invasion into Heaven. He not only led one-third of the angels of God who rebelled with him, but the pre-Adamite races he ruled over as well. The pre-Adamites had to have been a part of it or God would not have destroyed them. All this had to be before Adam's day for no such things have occurred since Adam was created.

In Luke 10:18, Jesus taught the fall of Satan from Heaven; after Lucifer's rebellion his name was changed to Satan. He fell because of pride and wanting to exalt his earthly kingdom over God's. This pride included not only pride in his beauty but in his great knowledge and power. The people he ruled had to be as corrupt as he to agree to be led by him to overthrow God. Their knowledge and advanced technology filled them with a corresponding pride and caused their ultimate destruction, which also included that of all the creatures that lived on the planet.

Scientists will attest to the fact that the Earth suffered a sudden cataclysmic event that killed everything in a day. Beasts found frozen in the ice still had the vegetation they were feeding on in their mouths, showing death came suddenly and without warning. This interplanetary war between Heaven and Earth was short and devastating. The evidence bears that out. The Earth still carries the scars.

The other evil angels who ruled planets elsewhere must have taught those civilizations the same technology as was taught here. These UFOs are probably from many different places in the universe, and yet they all seem to have similar designs and abilities. Even the beings that have been seen are sometimes similar in appearance to each other. The number of fingers, height, and sometimes color may vary, but the overall appearance is similar.

We are the ones who are different. God did that on purpose. He said, *"Let us make man in Our image"*. He made us of the dust of the Earth and yet created us only a little lower than the angels. He is very specific about what we are made of. We have no way of knowing what 'dust' these other people are made of.

When Adam was created he was given dominion over the Earth and over all creation. One can only guess at the jealousy and hatred this stirred up in Satan, who was determined to regain control over what he considered to be his property. Adam and Eve soon succumbed to his temptation and Adam lost his dominion to the Earth's original ruler. God in His great mercy has provided us with a second Adam. Christ became the second Adam and in defeating Satan regained dominion of the Earth. Those who trust in, believe in, and have faith in who Christ is and what He did share in that dominion. The final segment of this complete dominion is still in the future and will be covered in a later chapter.

The Earth was destroyed by meteors, earthquakes, erupting volcanoes, and a devastating and total flood and by a deep impenetrable darkness. This latter must have been caused by a covering of thick clouds, which would have caused temperatures too cold to support life.

The significance of actual findings of science regarding prehistoric animals and man, the age of the earth, its rock formations, and other facts can be realized only if we believe the bible's revelation of a pre-Adamite social system.

It is evident that many fossils came from a great catastrophe, being entombed in the strata instead of being slowly buried by sedimentation over millions of years. Historians tell us that the Earth has undergone one great and indescribable catastrophe such as what happened during the first destruction and flooding of the Earth. Such a shaking up of the entire Earth as well as the Flood could have caused many fossils to become deeply submerged.

The arctic regions give clear evidence of sudden calamity. In their extensive fields of fossilization and frozen mammoths, where multitudes of giant creatures have been found, some have been discovered with their stomachs filled with undigested food and in some instances with food also in their mouths. This shows they were feeding quietly when the crisis came and that they were destroyed suddenly. Apparently the arctic regions had tropical climate when these beasts were destroyed, for they had tropical food in their mouths. They had to have been 'fast frozen' when God kept the sun, moon and stars from shining on the Earth. Jeremiah 4:23-26 refers to the pre-Adamite destruction: *"I beheld the Earth, and lo, it was without form and void and heavens they had no light. I beheld, and lo, there was no man, and all the birds of the heavens were fled. I beheld, and lo, the fruitful place was a wilderness, and all the cities thereof were broken down at the presence of the Lord, and by His fierce anger."*

The following list summarizes points that prove this refers to the chaos of the original Earth:
1) It was without form and void (desolate and empty)
2) There was no light.
3) The mountains trembled and the hills moved lightly.
4) There was no man.
5) All the birds fled.
6) The fruitful places were a wilderness.
7) The cities were broken down at the presence of the Lord, and by his fierce anger.

The only time the Earth has ever been without form and void was when it was made chaos through the fall of Lucifer and the pre-Adamites and before the six days of Genesis 2:3 -2, 25. God brought the first great universal flood upon the Earth to destroy all life. (Genesis 1:2 and 2 Peter 3:5-8)

The only time the sun, moon, and stars were forbidden to give light on the Earth was in the period before the six days of recreation. There had been light on the earth when it was first created, 'in the beginning', and there has been light ever since the first day of the six days of recreation, so the period of the darkness was on the Earth sometime after the beginning and before the restoration of the Earth to a second habitable state. During the six days of recreation, permanent and eternal laws were given to the sun, Moon and stars as stated in the Bible. (Jeremiah 31:35-36; Genesis 1:14-19; Psalms 72:5, 17; and Psalms 89:35-37)

The mountains and hills have been moved and will again be moved by earthquakes, but there has never been a time since Adam to this day, nor will there ever be, a time from our day into all eternity when the Earth will be without a man, bird, or fruitful place, no matter what so many doomsayers would have us to believe.

We can see that there were men, birds and fruitful places on the Earth before Adam's time that were destroyed by the flood of Genesis 1:2 and 2 Peter 3:5-8. The Earth was created to be inhabited (Isaiah 48:18); it was inhabited from the beginning by people who lived in cities. There were nations and social systems of beings that were mortal and therefore capable of being drowned. They were beings that Adam could replace, for he was commanded to replenish the Earth. One thing is certain, Jeremiah 4:23-26 could not apply to the time of Noah, for at that time, the heavens had lights, and there were men, birds and fruitful places left on the Earth after the Flood, whereas because of the curse brought upon the original Earth, none of these things remained.

In Noah's Flood, God did not make a full end as He did in the First Flood. There are several contrasts between the two floods:

FIRST FLOOD	NOAH'S FLOOD
Earth made waste	Not made waste
Earth made empty	Not made empty
Earth made totally dark	Not dark
No light from heaven	Still had light
No days	Still had day and night
All vegetation was destroyed	Still had vegetation left
Waters off Earth in one day	Water took months to recede
All fish destroyed	Only land animals
No birds left	Birds preserved
No animals left	Animals preserved
No social system	Still had social system
Cause: Fall of Satan (Isaiah 14:12)	Cause: Wickedness of man and fallen angels (Gen.6:1-4)
No ark made to save	Noah's Ark saved life
Result: became necessary to make new fish, fowl, animals, man and vegetation	Result: no new creation needed to be made, for all things were preserved

This first creation must have gone from great spiritual enlightenment to the pit of spiritual darkness to have suffered such a fate along with Lucifer. Technological growth can never take the place of spiritual growth, which was God's purpose for creation. This was not Lucifer's purpose, however.

His purpose since he chose rebellion has always been to cause all of God's creation to worship himself instead of God. He found ways to eliminate anyone or anything getting in his way of obtaining this purpose. His goal has not changed. Without God, we have no defense from such a powerful being.

It should come as no surprise that Lucifer returned to the Earth after his devastating defeat and moving with envy and jealousy brought about the downfall of the new Earth ruler, Adam. Why all this desire to usurp man's dominion on Earth, if the Earth was not where Lucifer once ruled?

What has all this got to do with UFOs? Everything! Since Adam lost his dominion over the Earth, the race of man has become a teaching tool to the rest of the universe in how God deals with the creation He loves. In 1 Corinthians 4:9, it says: *"We are made a spectacle unto the world, (universe) and to angels and to men."* But, there are other reasons why we are made a spectacle. Those reasons will be dealt with throughout this book. Keep in mind that we are made in His image. God is very specific on that point!

There is no way of knowing how long the Earth remained without form and void between the two creations. It could have been millions of years, which would account for the great age of the Earth according to carbon dating and rock strata.

Man is the newcomer in the universe. The race of man has only been in existence for six thousand years as compared to the possible millions of years of existence that other races of the universe have lived.

Why are they so fascinated by the Earth and its inhabitants? Earth is the site of the greatest war between good and evil ever fought and will be again.

Chapter 3:

All the Giants Must Die

Greek mythology tries to give us a true picture of races of giants and their fathers who were the fallen angels they referred to as gods. Mythology is the outgrowth of tradition, memories, and legends, telling of the acts of these supernatural fathers and their offspring. Even before Noah's Flood, the Earth was filled with fallen angels and giants, but all record of them was destroyed in the Flood. It was because of their terrible evil and contamination of the human race that God flooded the Earth in Noah's time.

The legends and myths handed down to us are from the time after the Flood to when the fallen angels were cast into a special compartment of hell called Tartarus, along with those who had been chained there from the time before Noah's Flood. The giants were half mortal and half evil angels. They had to die; for once again their race was contaminating the race of man through whom the Son of God would someday be born.

The legends of Hercules, Zeus, Apollo, Neptune, and all the dwellers of Mount Olympus as well as the Cyclops and other monsters are all outgrowths of stories handed down through the time of these evil angels who were regarded as gods and their cohabitation with human women. Even before Noah's Flood, in Genesis 6:2, it says that *"the sons of God saw the daughters of men that they were fair, and they took them wives of all they chose."*

In Genesis 6:5-6, it says: *"There were giants in the earth in those days; and also after that, when the sons of god came in unto the daughters of men, and they bore children to them. The same became mighty men, men of renown. And God saw that the wickedness of man was great in the earth and that every imagination of the thoughts of his heart was only evil continually. And it repented the Lord that He had made man on the earth, and it grieved Him at His heart."*

The evil of man at that time was not just his own, but mingled with the horrible evil of those fallen angels who had compounded their sins by cohabiting with human women and contaminating the seed of man. This sin was in addition to their original rebellion with Lucifer before Adam.

In 2 Peter 2:4, it says: *"For if God spared not the angels that sinned, but cast them down to hell and delivered them into chains of darkness, reserved unto judgment."*

I am mentioning this verse to show the degree of evil these angels had committed.

The Jewish historian Josephus states, *"Many angels of God accompanied with women, and begat sons that proved unjust, and despisers of all that was good, on account of their own strength. These men did what resembled the acts of those whom the Grecians called, giants."* Again Josephus said, *"There was still then left the race of giants, who had bodies so large, and countenances (faces) so entirely different from other men, that they were surprising (or*

18

shocking) to the sight, and terrible to the hearing. The bones of these men are still shown to this very day." Josephus, BOOK OF ANTIQUITES, vol.2, page 142 and vol. 8, page 85 and 275.

Both the Old and New Testaments of the Bible teach that some angels committed sex sins and lived contrary to nature. In addition to the Scriptures already mentioned, Jude verses 6 and 7 say: *"The angels who kept not their first estate, but left their own habitation he hath reserved under darkness unto the judgment of the great day."* In Matthew 22:30, it states: *"In the resurrection they neither marry nor are given in marriage but are as the angels of God in Heaven."* The purpose of this verse is to show that human men and women who have a part in the resurrection will not marry, nor will they need to, in order keep their kind in existence. In the resurrected state, they live forever. Procreation will not be necessary. Neither has it ever been necessary for the angels, for they were created without number in the first place, whereas the race of man started with one pair, Adam and Eve.

There are no female angels on record. It makes sense to say then that the female was created specifically for the human race in order that it be kept in existence. All angels were created males as their kind is kept in existence without the reproductive process. Angels were created in vast numbers to begin with. Those numbers can never be depleted.

There are two classes of fallen angels; those loose with Satan who will be cast down to Earth during the future judgment (Revelations 12:7-12) and those who are now bound in hell for committing what the Bible calls fornication.

If the angels now bound in hell had not committed the sin of fornication in addition to the original sin of rebellion, they would still be loose with Satan. That theirs had been a sex sin is clear from 2 Peter 2:4 and Judges Verses 6 and 7, which identifies this class of fallen angels as the sons of God in Genesis 6:1-4.

The very purpose of Noah's Flood was to destroy the giant offspring of these angels, known as the sons of God, who committed fornication with the daughters of men. Think about it. How could a mortal human female have resisted these angels? They had to be the epitome of what we today would call 'hunks!' To consort with a god was probably considered a great honor.

Perhaps some of the huge stone architecture so carefully and faultlessly fitted together and still standing was built by these fallen angels and their giant offspring. Science can't figure out to this day how these structures could have been built, no matter how much slave power was employed. This would go a long way toward an explanation. A supernatural being would not need machines. They probably floated building materials into place. Some of the structures seen under the sea in the Bermuda Triangle area of the coast of Bimini could be possible remnants of a pre-Noah's Flood civilization. Atlantis may be a legend, but the possibility of such an advanced civilization is not so improbable, considering the supernatural nature of the inhabitants. Structures built after the

Flood are similar due to the fact that the builders were of the same nature as those before the Flood.

Scripture tells us that angels have charge of certain areas of the earth and sea. Legends of Neptune may not be far from the truth. His dominion was the sea. In Scripture there are evil angels who have charge over different rivers. They will be loosed to do evil during the Tribulation.

There is a constant between the angels of light and the evil angels. The prayers of Christians enable the angels of light to be victorious. Frank Peretti's books, THIS PRESENT DARKNESS, and PIERCING THE DARKNESS, illustrate how these wars are constantly going on around us and what part we play in them.

Satan came within eight people of accomplishing his purpose before Noah's Flood. The verse in Genesis that describes Noah as being perfect in his generations was not only referring to Noah's relationship to God, but to the fact that his family alone was free from the contamination of the seed of the fallen angels and giants.

Satan's near success must have gone to his head. When God promised Noah that he would never destroy the Earth with a flood again, Satan dared to try the same plan. After all it did almost succeed the first time. The second try had even greater chances to be successful since God could not destroy the contaminated seed without also destroying the race of man along with them or so Satan thought.

Satan's goal was to contaminate the race of man so the son of God could not be born. The Middle East area, especially the land known as Canaan, was filled with these evil races of giants. Then Joshua (Moses successor) sent out the twelve spies to spy out the land, as the Israelites were getting ready to take possession of the land as God had commanded them, ten spies brought back the bad report the inhabitants were giants and that they (the Israelites) were as grasshoppers in size by comparison. God wanted them to kill every single inhabitant. Because of their little faith, they failed to go in and totally conquer at the time, as God wanted them to do. It took much longer then it would have, had they done what God had told them in the first place.

Many unenlightened people of today think the God of the Old Testament was a cruel and bloody god, but the evil of these fallen angels and giants had filled the Earth again. God worked through the promise never to send a flood again. If they had not destroyed them, Jesus would never have been born and man would not have a Savior and those giants and fallen angels would still be dominating the Earth.

God commanded His people not to intermarry with them or be contaminated by their religions, some of which are still with us today in one form or the other. Since these creatures were all over the then occupied Earth before earthquakes and other natural disasters changed the locations of continents and continental bridges, the similarity of religions, structures, and legends at different regions of the Earth becomes easier to understand.

The following is the definition listed under 'giant' in the UNGER'S BIBLE DICTIONARY: *GIANT: an abnormally tall and powerful human of ancient Bible lands; the rendering of several Hebrew words.*

Nephilim: Numbers 13:33: *The form of the Hebrew word denotes a plural verbal adjective or noun of passive signification certainly from -napal- 'to fall', so that the connotative is the 'fallen ones.'*

Clearly meaning the unnatural offspring that were on the earth in the years before the flood, *"and also afterward, when the sons of God came into the daughters of men, and they bore children to them"* (Genesis 6:4). They mention the great statures of the Nephilim, the sons of Anak, in the evil report that the ten spies brought of the land of Canaan. They were exceedingly wicked and violent so that *"every intent"* of the thoughts of the men's hearts *"was only evil continually"* (Genesis 6:5)

Rephaim: The aboriginal giants who inhabited Canaan, Edom, Moab, and Ammon. In Abraham's time, 1950 B.C. Chedorlaomer defeated them. At the period of the conquest, 1440 B.C., Og, king of Bashan, is said to have alone remained of this race (Deuteronomy 3:11; Joshua 12:4, 13:12). His huge bedstead of iron is mentioned in particular.

Anakim: ("sons of Anak") In Numbers 13:33 the Anakim are classified with the Nephilim on account of their gigantic size.

Enim: A race that inhabited the country of the Moabites (Genesis 14:5) and that is pictured as great, numerous and tall as the Anakim. (Deuternonmy 2:10)

Much has been made of the Nephilim in recent times. They were just another race of evil giants. The word is used incorrectly in most instances.

Other references - From a remnant of the Anakim in Philistine Gath came the famous Goliath. (1 Samuel 17:40) Two of the Philistine giants are mentioned in 2 Samuel 21:16-22. If one reads on you will find that all of Goliath's family were eventually killed by King David and his men, numbering five in all.

The tradition of a giant race persisted in the ancient Near East and goes back in the Genesis account to intercourse between fallen angels and mortal women. Although this so-called angel hypothesis of Genesis 6: 1-4 is disclaimed by many Bible students, it is a clear implication of the original, says W.F. Albright, "

Yahweh was believed to have created astral as well as terrestrial beings and the former were popularly called, "the host of heaven" or "the sons of God." In Genesis 6:1, for example, the (astral) gods had intercourse with mortal women who gave birth to heroes, an idea that may often be illustrated from Babylonian and Greek mythology! But the Israelite who had this section recited, unquestionably thought of intercourse between angels and woman".

This explains why God commanded Israel to kill

them, everyone, even to the last man, woman and child. It also explains why he destroyed all the men women and children except for Noah and his family, at the time of the Flood.

This too answers skeptics questions regarding why the children were taken away with the adults in the Flood. God had to do away with this corruption entirely in order to fulfill His eternal plan and give the world its promised Redeemer, Jesus Christ. Jesus Christ the Redeemer has come now, and so Satan is reserving his forces for one last stand at the second coming of Christ.

It was the purpose of Satan and his fallen angels to corrupt the human race and thereby do away with pure Adamite stock through which Christ the Redeemer would come. This would avert their own doom and make it possible for Satan and his kingdom to keep control of the planet Earth indefinitely. It was said to Adam and Eve that the seed of the woman, Jesus, would defeat Satan and restore man's dominion. (Genesis 3:15)

If God had not destroyed all the giants with the flood and through conquest by the Israelites, we would still be living in a world filled with giants and their evil fathers. We have been allowed to choose our own destiny; a privilege we would never have had if these beings still existed.

The best physical evidence of their one time rule and existence the giant stones of ancient architecture put there by these evil giants and their supernatural fathers.

There are evil human men, but, there are also good men. There were no good giants. All were evil. That is another reason all the giants had to die.

Chapter 4:

The Five Compartments of Hell

The first compartment of hell is called Tartarus. It is where the fallen angels that have sinned before and after the Flood are bound in chains. All those so called gods, like Zeus and Apollo and their giant and monstrous offspring are there.

The second prison section is called Hell. It was, still is, and will continue to be the place where all the wicked human souls from Cain to the end of the Millennium go. Then at that time, all the wicked souls will be liberated out of this prison and will be given immortal bodies and be judged after the Millennium at the Great White Throne judgment before being cast into the Lake of Fire forever (Revelations 20:11-15, 21;8) This will be after the Millennium.

The third prison is the abyss or bottomless pit. It is the dwelling place of demons and certain angelic beings. No human being ever goes to the abyss. The Old Testament equivalent is Abaddon and is translated as 'destruction' in Job 26:5,6; 28:22; 31:12. The abyss is an immeasurable depth. It is a very deep chasm in the lower parts of the Earth. It is translated 'deep' in Luke 8:26-31; Romans 10:7, and 'bottomless pit' in Revelations 9:1-3, 11; 11:7; 17:8; 20:10. These Scriptures are further proofs that there are prisons in the lower parts of the Earth for departed spirits.

The fourth prison is called the Lake of Fire. This department is the eternal hell and perdition of wicked men, demons, fallen angels, and all rebellious creatures who have ever rebelled against God. It is called the Gehenna of Fire and is always translated 'hell'. (Matthew 5:22, 29, 30; 10:28; 18:9; 23:15, 33; Mark 9:43; Luke 12:5; James 3:6).

Instead of the final state penitentiary, we might call it the final penitentiary of the universe. The sentence here is for all of eternity. There will be no pardons, appeals, or parole. There will be an opening from the first hell to the surface during the Millennium so all will be able to see what happens to rebels. One of the openings will be the original site of the city of Babylon. The opening will be changed to the Lake of Fire after the Great White Throne Judgment so that all will be able to view the fate of rebels throughout all eternity.

The fifth compartment is called Paradise (Luke 16:19-31, 23:43). It is a place of comfort, water, and bliss. It was where the righteous souls and spirits lived after leaving their bodies at physical death. All the righteous went into this prison and were held captive by the devil against their will (Hebrews 2:14,15; Ephesians 4:7-11). The devil had the power of death and of the underworld before Christ conquered him. (Colossians 2:14-17; Revelations 1:18) It was into this prison that Jesus went to on the day he died. Luke 23:43, Matthew 12:40, Ephesians 4:7-11 make it clear that Paradise is located in the heart and lower parts of the Earth. Christ not only went into his prison, but He also went into Tartarus and preached to the angels. In fact, He conquered death, hell and the grave during his crucifixion and during the three days He was in the underworld. He rescued all the righteous souls who were in Paradise and took them to Heaven when he ascended on high. He now has the keys of hell and death. Ever since that time, the righteous go directly to Heaven (2 Corinthians 5:8; Phillippians 1:21-35; Hebrews 12:23; and Revelations 6:9,11).

Paradise is now empty. Or is it? There is a chance it is now being used by others. This will be covered in another chapter.

Chapter 5:

Vanished!

The earth is believed to be five and a half billion years old and middle aged by celestial standards. Further it is believed that if man ever reached other planets, he might find himself just a primitive and comparatively new in existence considering other beings on other planets. Planets are invisible to terrestrial telescopes because they are cold masses, emitting no light of their own. One thing is certain. The Bible does teach that the heavens are now inhabited (2 Chronicles 18:18; Nehemiah 9:6; Job 25:3; Daniel 4:35; Matthew 22:30; Luke 2:13, 14; Ephesians 1:14, 15; Colossians: 16, 17; Revelations 12:12, 13:6, and 19:14).

In Isaiah 18:3, it says: *"All ye inhabitants of the world, and dwellers on the earth, se ye, and when He lifteth up an ensign on the mountains and when Be bloweth a trumpet, hear ye."*

Psalms 33:8 says: *"Let all the earth fear the Lord; let all the inhabitants of the world stand in awe of Him."*

In Phillippians 2:10, it says, *"That at the name of Jesus EVERY knee must bow, in HEAVEN, and EARTH, and UNDER the earth."*

We already know this includes angels, demons, and men but when God says ALL, He means all. God is speaking as though dwellers of another world are here. God knows about them; otherwise, how could they (aliens) see Him on our mountains. Having established that God Himself tells us the universe is inhabited and that there are observers, visitors, and intruders here above the Earth, on the Earth, and under the Earth, let us consider the strange happenings in the Bermuda Triangle.

The Bermuda Triangle is an area that includes the sea off the eastern coast of Florida, extending to and including Bermuda, the Sargasso Sea, the Bahamas, and the area near the coast of Puerto Rico. The Sargasso Sea has also been referred to as "the Doldrums."

Many experiences of strange sightings and disappearances over the years are documented in detail in Charles Berlitz's book, WITHOUT A TRACE. He states:

"there seems to be no unifying factor with possibly one rather disquieting exception in considering the question whether in the case of planes that vanish from the sky, surface craft that disappear without a trace at sea, and the cases of passengers and crew (but not cargoes) that vanish from the decks of ships. There does seem to be one unifying and special ingredients in all three types of disappearance. This special ingredient is, apparently, human beings!

A considerable percentage of the shops have been found, but never the occupants. Even animals have been found on board some of the derelicts; a canary on one, a dog on another and two cats on another. None of these except for the fact that they were hungry, indicating that they had not been fed for an indeterminate period, were able to throw any light on the disappearances of passengers and crews."

Some of the same types of disappearances have been reported off the southeastern coast of Japan, which is on the exact opposite side of the Earth from the Bermuda Triangle. Both places report the same happenings:

- Compass and instruments malfunction
- Time is lost or gained
- Unusual wave action consisting not only of tidal waves but holes and hills in and on the surface of the sea is observed.
- Another special attribute of luminous white water is noted.
- Unexpected modification of our accepted laws concerning matter, gravity, space, and time are reported.

Many flying saucers have been seen in these areas and are observed deliberately disappearing beneath the surface of the sea. Ghost ships from the past have been seen and reported by many, the most common of which is the FLYING DUTCHMAN.

The magnetic fields that surround UFOs coupled with the strong planetary magnetic fields in that area may cause reemergence of some of these scenes from the past and even conversations from the past that are there one moment and gone the next. Some theorize that scenes, words, and strong emotions are indelibly recorded in time and can be picked up at different times and locations. God has said that we will answer for every idle word spoken and everything done while in this life. Considering these "glimpses" into the past and ghostly manifestations this should not be so hard to believe.

A curious legend has arisen, based on the over flight of the South Pole accomplished by Admiral Byrd in 1929. It concerns a radio report allegedly broadcast by Admiral Byrd while in flight, a report so incredible that it was officially silenced. It concerns a sighting made by Admiral Byrd while in the vicinity of the Pole.

Admiral Byrd suddenly emerged from a fog and found himself flying over a land free of ice and was able to distinguish vegetation, lakes, and what seemed to be animals resembling mammoths or huge buffalo and also men in the vicinity of the animals. He is said to have said, *"Look! Do you see it? There is grass down there. The grass is lush. How green it is! There are flowers all over and look at the animals. They look like elk. The grass is growing up to their bellies. There are people, too. They seem surprised to see a plane."*

Some researchers have suggested Admiral Byrd penetrated a time warp after passing through areas of intense magnetism. While it is generally accepted that Admiral Byrd saw something unusual during his flight over both poles, a legend has arisen, suggested perhaps by ancient beliefs that there are great caverns within the earth (or that the Earth itself is hollow) and that entrances to these caverns of inner Earth may exist at the somewhat flattened parts of the globe at the two poles.

These legends of an inner Earth are described in Hindu, Buddhist, and other religious literature and stories handed down through time. The inner Earth is described as the home of the demigods and men who occasionally ascend to the outer Earth. This Shangri La or Aghati (Paradise perhaps?) has ever been through the ages a constant object of quest by rulers, travelers, explorers, and mystics in Asia and elsewhere, and even Hitler, apprised of Aghati by some mystics in his service, at one time joined in the hunt and dispatched several teams to search for entrances to this secret hidden inner world.

Perhaps time windows are more common than one might think. Other facts that influence the bending of time may one day be discovered. The conditions of this bending may exist not only in outer space, as has been predicted by Einstein and others but even on certain parts of the earth's surface.

It is certainly possible and even probable that other more advanced alien technologies have this knowledge. There is evidence that our own government has experimented with magnetic force, attempting to use it as the ultimate camouflage during World War II.

In October of 1943, the U.S. Navy allegedly conducted a series of tests at the Philadelphia Navy Yard, at Newport News, Virginia, and at sea. Although a certain amount has been written about the Philadelphia Experiment in books, magazines, and other domestic and foreign newspapers as well as related in movies based on this event, basic sources of information remain clouded. Witnesses have died, other witnesses or informed personnel refuse to be quoted, and at least one researcher has committed suicide (so they say). Reports and comment persist that the Philadelphia Experiment had to do with an attempt to make a Navy ship disappear in a 1943 experiment that was eminently successful, except for the effects it had on the crew.

The connection between the Philadelphia Experiment and the Bermuda Triangle stems from the use of an artificially induced magnetic field to cause the temporary disappearance of a destroyer and its crew. The advantage, of course, was to cause the ultimate camouflage in invisibility to a warship and crew. Its importance to scientific theory is ever more profound: men and material were temporarily projected into another dimension.

When the experiment first began to take effect, a hazy green light became evident, something like reports we have from survivors of incidents in the Triangle who tell of a luminous greenish mist. Soon the whole ship was full of this green haze and the craft, together with its personnel, began disappearing from sight of those on the dock. As the force field intensified, some crew members began disappearing and had to be found by tactile contact and restored to visibility by a laying-on-of-hands technique. It was rumored that many were hospitalized, some died, and others were adversely affected mentally.

There are only a few of the original experimental crew left by now. Most went insane. One man just walked through the wall of his quarters in sight of his wife and child and two other crew members and was never seen again. Others periods of time when they would disappear and for even as long as six months would later reappear. During the time they were "frozen", they had no recollection of where they had been and felt they were in a comatose state. The Philadelphia Experiment was a complete success. The men were complete failures.

A copy of a book written by Dr. Jessup about this experiment and its results was handed back to him for examination. It was explained to him that the book had been sent by mail to Admiral F.N. Furth, in the summer of 1955 and had been examined by Navy Intelligence officers as well as by the Aeronautics Projects Office. The book was found to be filled with handwritten comments about Jessup's texts, apparently written by three people who had passed or sent the book, one to the other, and made their annotations in different colored inks.

The comments themselves unusual for several reasons:

1) The commentators or critical reviewers of the text seemed to assume the roles of representatives of a secret and ancient culture, having knowledge of previous scientific development on Earth and in the universe, of constant visits to Earth by interplanetary spacecraft and their means of travel (as well as references to their method of operation), and of an interplanetary war that had devastated Earth.
2) The comments were full of references to force fields, dematerialization, and present observation of Earth by great and small spaceships.

Dr. Jessup died unexpectedly and mysteriously in 1959, ending this research. I have no idea if it is still possible to get a copy of Dr. Jessup's book. It was called, THE CASE FOR THE UFO: ANNOTATED EDITION. It was published by Gray Barker, Clarksburg, West Virginia.

All these inter-dimensional shifts and time window theories and ideas can very confusing and frightening to most of us. God has promised there will always be linear time and that day, night, times and seasons will never cease from the Earth. Perhaps the Philadelphia experiment was a good lesson to show that man is not physically or mentally able to withstand inter-dimensional travel. If it ever develops, it will have to be at a time when God has prepared us for it.

When the Earth and atmospheric heavens are cleaned up by fire, perhaps these time windows and overlapping ghostly images and sounds from the past will be some of the things wiped away so man can start a new world clean of old memories and time traps, some of which were probably put there by some of these visitors from outer and inner space. Hold on to the promise that linear time is here forever. *"While the earth remaineth seed time and harvest, summer and winter, day and night shall not cease."* (Genesis 8:22)

Chapter 6:

Angels of Light

Only three angels are mentioned by name in the Bible. In the army of angels, they are the generals. There is Michael, who fights for Israel, see the book of Daniel; Gabriel, who announces great events; and Lucifer, the one who became Satan.

The angelic beings known as 'common angels' are the most numerous. They are intelligent, wise, patient, meek, joyful, powerful, mighty, and obedient. They are heavenly spirit beings; not demons, not human. Limited in knowledge, higher than men and are always spoken as male beings, not as being sexless as some teach. They have wills, spirit bodies with all bodily parts and passions as do men.

They do not need rest or food, they can appear visible and invisible, and can operate in the physical realm, and can travel at inconceivable speed. They can speak languages and do all things men can do.

They all have special work to do. They drive spirit horses, guard gates, wage war in actual bodily combat, execute judgments, rule nations, sing praise and worship God. They lead sinners to gospel workers, direct preachers, appear in dreams, bind Satan, guard the abyss, re-gather Israel, separate the good and bad, bring answers to prayers, and do many other things for God and man.

Many times throughout Scripture, God Himself appears as an angel to speak to people. He came to Abraham to announce he would soon have a son in one instance. His walking with the three Hebrew children in the fiery furnace is another example.

Angels look like men in appearance, so one never knows if one has entertained angels unaware. Perhaps they are best known as guardian angels which attend to and protect those who believe and put their trust in God. They are there to intervene when we pray to God for help, or when others pray for us. (1 Kings 19:5 -7; Daniel 6:22; Matthew 4:11; Acts 10; Hebrews 1:14)

They were created by God before the Earth. They are not to be worshipped. They are organized into principalities and powers with thrones. (Colossians 1:16, 2:16; Roman 8:38; Ephesians 6:10-18; 1 Peter 3:22) They are subject to God and are interested in earthly affairs.

Many people have had experiences with angels, whether visible or invisible. Perhaps the man who held you back at just the right moment to keep you from stepping in front of an oncoming vehicle and then disappeared was an angel, or the airline ticket agent who told you over the phone there were no more seats available on a certain flight of a plane that crashed. Perhaps it was an angel's voice that told you to take a different way home and you obeyed, finding out later that the road you would have taken had been washed out and several had been caught in the waters and drowned. Almost all people that belong to God can name at least one experience of this type.

When I was eight years old, my parents took me to the beach. I didn't know how to swim, but loved to collect all the interesting items one finds on a beach, both in and out of the water. I kept going out farther and farther with my head under water most of the time scanning the bottom for treasures. Before I knew it, I had wandered out farther than I had intended and could not get my head above the water.

Suddenly a hand got me by the hair and pulled me up. A big man with a dark tan told me to get back to my parents, do as they told me, and not wander out so far. I was too scared to argue. I got out of the water. I looked back to see where the man was, but there was no sign of him anywhere. I stayed on shore for a while, watching to see if he had ducked under the water, but I never saw him again.

A couple of years later, I was taking a short-cut home from school near a little stream. All I remember is that two older boys started following me, giggling and jostling each other. I got scared and started to run. They caught up with me, pushed me down, and dragged me to the stream, holding my head under the water. One was sitting on me, and the other was helping to hold my head down. It seemed like an eternity had gone by and I was in a panic. Suddenly the weight on my back and the hands disappeared and as I came up gasping for air, I saw something disappearing out of sight at the edge of my peripheral vision and the two boys running for their lives. I never actually saw what had scared those boys off. I just ran home, glad to be alive and sobbing with relief.

All through my childhood, there were so many occasions when I could have died or at least been seriously hurt that I can't even remember them all.

One of the occasions I was driving. It was night and everyone else in the car was asleep. Interstate I-90 was in the process of being constructed. I heard a very loud, distinct, and familiar voice calling me by name and telling me to wake up. I woke up just in time to put on the brakes before going through a barricade and landing us all in a river. When I thought about it later, I kept trying to place the voice. It was familiar but, I never could identify it.

Fairly recently there were nine of us in a car headed for church which was a few miles away. We were cruising along at 65 miles per hour. Something hit us on the right side, setting us into a spin that landed us in the sand of an embankment next to the road. We then saw a red sports car take off and disappear. This car had not been behind us. No one could figure out where it had come from. We were in an area of the interstate that was near the exit where Satanic rituals were rumored to go on all the time. At any rate no one was hurt. We managed to push the car out of the sand and continued on to our destination with the right rear side of the car all dented. For our car to be hit from that side, someone would have had to come up out of the embankment to hit us.

God's 26 Guards

Here's a message that will bring you chills. Have you ever felt the urge to pray for someone

41

and then just put it on a list and say, "I'll pray for them later?" Or has anyone ever called you and said, "I need you to pray for me, I have this need?" Read the following story that was sent to me and may it change the way that you may think about prayer and also the way you pray. You will be blessed by this....

A missionary told this true story while visiting his home church in Michigan. "While serving at a small field hospital in Africa, every two weeks I traveled by bicycle through the jungle to a nearby city for supplies. This was a journey of two days and required camping overnight at the halfway point. On one of these journeys, I arrived in the city where I planned to collect money from a bank, purchase medicine, and supplies, and then begin my two-day journey back to the field hospital. Upon arrival in the city, I observed two men fighting, one of whom had been seriously injured. I treated him for his injuries and at the same time talked to him about the Lord. I then traveled two days, camping overnight, and arrived home without incident. Two weeks later I repeated my journey. Upon arriving in the city, I was approached by the young man I had treated. He told me that he had known I carried money and medicines. He said, 'Some friends and I followed you into the jungle, knowing you would camp overnight. We planned to kill you and take your money and drugs. But just as we were about to move into your camp, we saw that you were surrounded by 26 armed guards. At this, I laughed and said that I was certainly all alone in that jungle campsite. The young man pressed the point, however, and said, 'No, sir, I was not the only person to see the guards, my friends also saw

42

them, and we all counted them. It was because of those guards that we were afraid and left you alone.' At this point in the sermon, one of the men in the congregation jumped to his feet and interrupted the missionary and asked if he could tell him the exact day this happened. The missionary told the congregation the date, and the man who interrupted told him this story: *"On the night of your incident in Africa, it was morning here and I was preparing to go play golf. I was about to putt when I felt the urge to pray for you. In fact, the urging of the Lord was so strong; I called men in this church to meet with me here in the sanctuary to pray for you. Would all of those men who met with me on that day stand up?"*

The men who had met together to pray that day stood up. The missionary wasn't concerned with who they were, he was too busy counting how many men he saw. There were 26!

This story is an incredible example of how the Spirit of the Lord moves. If you ever hear such prodding, go along with it. Nothing is ever hurt by prayer except the gates of hell.

What most people do not realize is that there is a constant war going on around us that we cannot even see, but that directly affects us. Demons are the ones who kill, steal, and destroy. The angels of light are fighting on our behalf. The cast of characters that inhabit this planet, both visible and invisible is so vast that, if we were to be aware of them all, one would be unable to live a normal life for all the distractions.

Many people can tell stories of miraculous escapes from death and injury and of having the feeling that God was intervening directly on their behalf. God's angels stay busy looking after those who belong to God and those who are being prayed for. Prayer is our most powerful weapon.

The faithful angels and the saints of God will be helping God to administer the affairs of the universe from the Earth, which is to be the eternal headquarters of His government. (Revelations 21:2; Ephesians 2:7; 3:11)

The Millennium is not the end of it all, but only the beginning. During the Millennium the natural descendants of Adam will learn to live according to God's laws. Those who are still in rebellion, even without the influence of Satan and his cohorts, by the end of that time will join with Satan as he is loosed out of the abyss where he has been chained for the thousand years of the Millennium. These people will go with him in one last battle against God and His people. During the battle the Earth and the heavens surrounding it will be cleansed by fire. The Earth can be cleansed by fire with the natural people of God still living here. By that I mean people who live in a natural physical body such as we have today can remain unharmed. This will be covered in a chapter called "Fire".

We will then have a new heaven and a new Earth that will remain in a state of perfection throughout all eternity. They have plans of their own.

Chapter 7:

Demons

Demons are disembodied spirits and do not seem to be able to operate in the material world except through possession of men and beasts that have bodies for them to utilize. Satan and the fallen angels have angelic bodies and cannot enter bodily into anyone. The demons are subject to the higher ranking fallen angels.

It is thought by some that the demons are the evil departed spirits of the pre-Adamite civilization. There is no Scripture to prove this. It is in the book of Enoch, however, that civilization was made up of the hybrid offspring of fallen angels and human women and was repeated again prior to the flood of Noah.

What is the real nature of demons? They are evil, intelligent, powerful, disembodied spirits (Revelations 16:13-16); not angel nor human; for they possess men and can be cast out and are individuals. They have knowledge, faith, feelings, and fellowship. They have doctrines, wills, and miraculous powers.

Demons have jobs to do. They possess people and can cause dumbness, deafness, blindness, lunacy, mania, uncleanness, supernatural strength, suicide, lust counterfeit worship, error, sickness, disease, lying enchantment, witchcraft, false doctrines, and every evil thing they can possibly do to God and man.

They can teach, fight, get mad, tell fortunes (i.e. they rule Ouija boards), be friendly (called familiar spirits), and imitate departed dead. They can cause ghostly manifestations. They can also cause people to remember 'past lives'. Such demons that were familiar with these people of the past have long memories.

They are possessed of more than ordinary intelligence. Their rightful place is in the abyss. They have personality, are disembodied, are Satan's emissaries, and can enter into and control both men and beasts and seek embodiment. There is a difference between demon possession and demon influence. Perhaps a good illustration of demon influence would be something similar to those old cartoons that showed a little devil sitting on a character's shoulder, whispering into his ear enticing him to do the wrong thing.

Demons know their fate and that of those who have power over them. They fear God, inflict physical maladies, war on saints, and influence men. All unbelievers are afflicted or possessed by them.

There are demon spirits for every sickness, unholy trait, and doctrinal error known among men. Faith in God and prayer are our best defense against them. They must be cast out by the power of God in order for the sufferers to get relief from them. Diseases, germs and virus are really living forms of corruption that come into the bodies of men in order to bring them death.

Communication with demon spirits is forbidden in both the Old and New Testaments of the Bible. Fallen angels and demons are all rebels connected with the planet Earth.

Chapter 8:

The Aerial Phenomenon

The mysterious aerial phenomenon, known as UFOs or flying saucers, have been seen in the skies over every country on Earth for an unknown number of years. During World War II and wars since, they have been dubbed 'Foo fighters' as they swooped through the skies during battles, confusing those who saw them into thinking the enemy had devised some new and mysterious secret weapon.

UFOs have been seen by millions worldwide. Some of the witnesses have been well-known, credible people in the military and scientific community.

At night UFOs appear as bright lights in the sky. These lights change color and shape at times and appear to wink out in one area and reappear in another. Sometimes they appear as a dull silver or pearly color. Some have been seen to be disk shaped. Other shapes are globular, wedged, winged, triangular, or bell shaped. Some hum, some are silent and seem to create a vacuum beneath them. They all travel at fantastic speeds, make abrupt stops, turns, and maneuvers that are impossible for any craft made by man.

Proving their existence is no longer necessary. So many men and women of impeccable reputation have documented the fact of their existence that it is only left to the reader to either believe it or not. There are some who will never believe until an alien lands on the White House lawn in full view of waiting video news cameras and says, "Take me to your leader!" People will believe what they are comfortable believing. For man it would be a serious threat to all their values, standards, and religious beliefs. The culture shock could be devastating.

As in the ancient past, when beings were observed to have extraordinary powers, they were thought of as gods. Even now it is no different. Some have gone so far as to build a religion around them.

The church community continues to ignore them or brush them off as another manifestation of angels, devils, or demons. Sometimes Ezekiel's wheels are referred to.

The July 1947 crash of a UFO at Roswell, New Mexico, started the modern day era of the influx of UFO sightings. This crash proves they are not angels, devils, or demons. Dead bodies of these aliens were seen by many witnesses. The fact that they can die proves they certainly are not supernatural nor do they deserve the title of god of anything. They merely have a superior technology and have been reported to have such command of magnetic force that they are capable of flying from the region of one star system to another. They can also levitate themselves, use mental telepathy, mind control, go through what we consider solid objects, affect Earth's power sources, and shape shift on occasion. These same powers were used by the fallen angels and their offspring in the past to frighten and control the physical humans who populate this planet. The main difference in the case of aliens is that these creatures need

ships to travel in and are mortal; not immortal
as angels and demons are.

There are several different types of aliens.
The ones most commonly reported are gray in
color, thin, three to four feet tall with large
heads, small noses, tiny mouths and huge eyes.
Others are more insect-like and are similar in
appearance to a praying mantis; some are described as reptilian. Some have hands with five
digits, others with three or four. Some hands
are webbed. Some have suction cups on the ends
of their fingers. Some have an undeveloped fe-
tus like appearance.

Apparently planet Earth has been entertaining
visitors from many different places. They have
been seen swooping down out of the skies and
coming up out oceans, lakes, and other bodies
of water. Many have been sighted in the Bermuda
Triangle area.

Some of the occupants of these ships from outer
and inner space have made no effort to conceal
their malevolence. Some have been deceptively
"kind," given their victims ominous messages,
and have shown their human specimens hybrid hu-
man/alien offspring. Some of their victims report increased clairvoyance, visions, and re-
curring spiritual messages.

They have been here a long, long time. In history references to trolls, fairies, little people, elves, and fairy ships were what we would
now refer to as UFOs and their occupants.

The reports of abduction started with Betty and
Barney Hill, who were abducted in September of

1961. They were living in New Hampshire at the time. There was a 1975 film called The Interrupted Journey, starring James Earl Jones as Barney. It was shown on television in the United States. The film was based on the true experiences of Betty and Barney. There have been many books and films on the subject of UFOs and the abduction experience since that time.

Animal mutilations have been attributed to UFO activity. Typically the animals are found with selected parts, such as eyes, tongue, sexual organs, udders, and pieces of skin missing. The cuts are made with surgical precision by an unknown instrument that burns. Sometimes all the blood is drained. There is no blood found on the ground near them.

Predators avoid the carcasses. No tracks of the mutilators are found, even when the ground is soft or covered with snow. Ranchers who depend on their cattle for their living are constantly frustrated and desperate for an answer. Their pleas to the government for help in solving the problem have gone unanswered.

The governments of the world know more than they let on. Perhaps some of the cover ups serve the purpose of hiding how helpless they are to do anything. Leaders may remain silent in exchange for whatever UFO technology these creatures 'let' them have and what they can derive from crashed UFOs.

Chapter 9:

Human/Alien Relationships

In Travis Walton's book, THE WALTON EXPERIENCE, an abductee, who to his knowledge was abducted only once, records his experiences and the effect it had on himself and on his friends. He states:

It is understandable that people would expect the seven of us to make a profound religious interpretation of the experience, or at least have a turning to God for an understanding that would lead to a personal spiritual revival for each of us. But this has not been the case. If anything there has been the exact reverse of that in some respects. The most religious member of our group, who was ordinarily an abstainer, took to smoking and drinking."

And later he goes on to say:

"All of us have had a slightly aimless turn to our lives. None of us have held a job very steadily since then. The reluctance to hire nuts has not been all of it either. The best I can do to describe the feelings is that of a stripped ego, a sort of lost feeling that permeates the entire being. Perhaps glimpsing the technological superiority of a distant civilization impresses us with our own lack of central importance in the overall scheme of things. We have been moved to closely reexamine all the basic ideas and standard by which we direct our lives. And in this examination we found them lacking in a totality of perspective. I have begun to believe that, in taking our eyes off the ground and thinking in

terms of the entire creation of space, we have discovered the chink in the armor of man's vanity; a challenge to his egocentric concepts of the world. Man, standing in clear view of the infinite universe, finds himself fighting an insistent feeling of INSIGNIFICANCE."

If these creatures from other dimensions, planets, star systems, or wherever they come from, can cause this reaction, they have already succeeded in one of their main purposes: to demoralize and break the spirit of the race of man and most importantly, to turn man away from God, who is his only source of power and his only defense against these intruders.

These creatures may not be fallen angels or demons, but they appear to have some of the same goals. However the July 1947 UFO crash at Roswell, New Mexico, proves these creatures may be well advanced beyond us in technology, but are still vulnerable enough to make mistakes. They can crash, burn and die. The fallen angels and demons do not have this weakness. These aliens have the advantage of superior techniques of mind control.

All through the years that abductions have been recorded, almost all abductees relate having eggs, semen, and even fetuses taken from them. It seems all these various aliens are now doing what fallen angels once did. They want to change genetically, evolve, and become a part of the race of man. Their approach is even more insidious and devious because some of these hybrids could be indistinguishable from anyone else.

Their 'victims' are left with posthypnotic messages of misinformation. The most common are these:

- Mankind is going to become sterile.
- They (the aliens) are physically related to man.
- They are DEPENDENT UPON MEN for the reproduction of their own species.
- They are conducting a genetic engineering program with Earth's life forms for preservation purposes.
- There will be a drastic shifting of the Earth's surface brought on by devastating earthquakes, diseases, wars, and other disasters in the near future.

This goes directly against what Scripture tells us. Man will never be sterile. God has promised us that there will be generations of men forever on the Earth.

These creatures are dependent upon us, not us upon them for survival. They need our seed. We do not need theirs. To understand why they need us refer to the chapter in this book called, Man's Dominion. The preservation of man is not under the jurisdiction of aliens. They are concerned with their preservation, not ours.

All this interest in ecology has been prevalent in just the past few years. Is this pressure to save the trees, spotted owls, the whales, and the ozone layer due to their influence? At the same time a devaluation of human life is taking place worldwide. Killing babies and the elderly is becoming more and more commonplace.

Can this fanatical interest in the ecology save us from earthquakes, meteors, tidal waves, and disease? Are we preserving all these creatures for us or for them? The aliens have admitted there will be a drastic depopulating of the Earth in the near future. No wonder they do not bother to just eliminate us all. It will be done for them by natural disaster, or so they think. Let us examine some of the results of human/alien contact:

- Loss of faith in God and a turning away from the Bible;
- Feeling the need to surrender control to something superior even though cruel;
- The 'don't fool with Mother Nature' syndrome causes many to become more concerned with the creation rather than the Creator;
- As stated earlier, warnings of impending doom;
- Intense feelings of vulnerability, helplessness, and separateness, being out of control and chronic fear;
- Those who are hybrids want the aliens to be in control. They feel themselves to be superior and believe it is their job to convince people to cooperate for their own good and the good of the planet;
- Many abductees are turning to New Age philosophy, Tibetan Buddhism and other religions that recognize and respect the encounters and spiritual awareness of the abductee;
- Others become victim to the ultimate deception and are turning from the Creator to worship of the creation, others gods and spirits;

- Abductees are beginning to consider their experiences as one of personal growth and ultimate enlightenment.

Not all victims succumb, as other comments have included the following: *"The beings try to reassure and say, 'Don't be afraid,' but that does not work. They are so full of lies! They have no respect for feelings or love or relationships."* Another described them as having big black eyes that do not blink. They are impressed that the aliens have the attitude that they are totally superior.

The depopulating of the Earth is already well known to any student of the Bible. It is described in great detail in the last book, called Revelation. It is also found in Isaiah, Ezekiel, Joel, and other books of the Old Testament. The first depopulation process will be the evacuation of God's people prior to the time when He judges the Earth and its people for their un-repented sins. This will be much like the instance when Lot, Abraham's nephew, was rescued from Sodom before God destroyed it because of the terrible sins committed there. The rest of the depopulation process will be via wars, earthquakes, starvation, disease, scorching from the sun, meteors, comets, predatory animals and demons from the abyss. The aliens are only telling us what has already been predicted in Scripture. Their version of the outcome is considerably different, however.

There is definitely to be a calling out or 'rapture' of God's believers before all the predicted calamities come upon the Earth. People will be deceived into believing that aliens have abducted them because they are interfering with 'progress' and the new world order. In fact, governments of the world will use this to bring in the new world order and the new one world religion, which will be a form of UFOlogy, proclaiming that the aliens are the ones who created our race and seeded this planet, thereby asserting themselves as gods and disclaiming God altogether as a supreme being. In fact, they will claim that Jesus Christ was one of them. Anyone reading the doctrine of Jesus will see the absolute contradiction of this. His teachings and all teachings of the Bible are in direct contradiction to their philosophy and claims.

There are those who would rather believe that they are only good for breeding stock rather than to believe all of us <u>ARE THE SUPERIOR RACE CHOSEN BY GOD TO RULE THE UNIVERSE WITH HIM!</u> We are lowering ourselves to merge with them. God's plan for man sounds too good to be true! The simplicity of the truth is a stumbling block for mankind. Many of us are like Naaman, a general in the Old Testament, (2 Kings 5:1-11) who was cured of leprosy by dipping seven times in the muddy Jordan River in obedience to what God's prophet, Samuel, told him. Being a soldier he had to be convinced that he did not have to do some mighty heroic deed to earn it. He almost lost his healing, because it was so difficult for him to believe the simplicity of the answer. The key was obedience to God no matter how silly it seemed.

Money, talent, and deed cannot buy a place in God's plan. One has to believe that Jesus is the Son of God, that what He says is true, and be willing to obey what He says. Instead most would rather believe a complicated lie and become something less, rather than believe the truth and help God rule the universe.

God wants one thing. Whether we are red, yellow, black or white does not matter as long as we are human and true descendants of Adam. Alien blood is absolutely unacceptable. The aliens think they can share our destiny if they are merged with us.

This is similar to the strategy that Satan used with the fallen angels: If the survivors are half human and half alien, God will have to settle for that. It seems the aliens are slow learners. If they know so much about our history, they have to know God will never allow that. Even aliens will only believe what they want to believe whether it is true or not!

The one world religion the aliens create will be defeated by the Antichrist in the middle of the Tribulation, when Satan changes his allegiance from them to his human representative on the Earth, so even they are victims of deception. All will succumb to the one world religion and later to the Antichrist, except for the Jews and those around the world who choose to follow God. These people will be persecuted mercilessly by the aliens, demons and the Antichrist as stated in Scripture.

There will be those from all nations who will survive and live in their natural bodies through the whole Millennium and forever. The alien's future is not so certain.

In Matthew 13:24-30 it says, *"Another parable put he forth unto them saying.* *"The Kingdom of heaven is likened unto a man which sowed good seed in his field; but while men slept, his enemy came and sowed tares among the wheat, and went his way. But when the blade was sprung up, and brought forth fruit, then appeared the tares also. So the servants of the householder came and said unto him, "Sir, didst not thou sow good seed in thy field? From whence then hath it tares?" He said unto them, "An enemy hath done this." The servant said unto him, "Wilt thou then that we go and gather them up?" But he said, "Nay; lest while ye gather up the tares, ye root up also the wheat with them Let both grow together until the harvest; and in the time of harvest I will say to the reapers, 'gather ye together first the tares, and bring them in bundles to burn them; but gather the wheat into my barn."*

These verses are most generally thought to mean evil men, but men are not born to be destroyed nor are they the spawn of the evil one. They choose to do this later when they grow old enough to make a choice. These are evil seeds from the beginning. This would seem to be an apt description of aliens and their genetic tampering. We may not be able to conquer these creatures, but God can and plans to do just that.

The physiological explanations of abduction are as follows: The nasal cavity, ears, eyes and genitals are of particular interest to aliens. Some abductees have described an object being inserted into the nostril and being able to hear a crushing sound as bone is penetrated.

Many have nosebleeds after this. Those subject to nasal problems now have a history of chronic sinusitis.

Documented evidence has shown that some abductees have been probed in their eyes and ears with a similar instrument. After this, some experience blindness, blurred vision, swollen watery, and painful eyes, and red irritated eyes.

Some scars that are apparent on many abductees also follow a pattern. Scars have been observed on the calf, thigh, hip, shoulder, knee, spinal column, and on the right side of the back and forehead. The scars fall into two basic groups. The first is a thin, straight, hairline cut, linear and about one to three inches long, and the second is a scoop-like or circular depression about one eighth to three quarters of an inch in diameter and perhaps as much as one quarter of an inch deep.

Other signs and symptoms commonly reported are:

- Tingling, prickling, or static electric shock sensations are felt over the skin, followed by paralysis of the entire body, except for the heart and lungs.
- Rashes are seen on the body, most appearing on the chest area and the lower extremities. Many are circular or otherwise geometrical in shape.
- Aliens have taken blood samples, eggs, sperm, and tissue scraping from ears, eyes, noses calves, thighs, and hips leaving evidence that all abductees are given some type of preparation prior to examination.

Some witnesses have received oral liquid medication, others an application of a preoperative type preparation over various parts of their bodies. They are also subjected to some type of twilight sleep state.

Even with all this, many times abductees suffer intense pain and terror during some procedures. Despite objections, the aliens appear to be indifferent to their victims pain and suffering.

Abductees are taken to different places. Some have reported leaving the ship and going into what appeared to be subterranean levels of our own planet, Earth.

One well-known abductee, Betty Andreasson Luca, reported a beautiful area with trees and water and several alien 'babies.' It was very peaceful there. She said that while there she was in an 'out of body' state, which the aliens had instigated technologically with a small device they carried on their belts.

If this area was underground and she in an 'out of body' state, it is possible she was in the area of hell called Paradise, which was deserted and left empty two thousand years ago when Christ took the righteous occupants to their permanent home in heaven. This is strictly a matter of conjecture on my part.

She also stated she saw what looked like angels guarding the entrance. They would have to have been fallen angels to have been party to such an occurrence as an abduction. Hell, as well as Paradise, is part of the underworld included in Satan's rule. God does not coerce, manipulate, cause pain, anguish, or terror, nor do His angels.

God is a respecter of man's free will. He does not need to abduct or conduct experiments. Why would the Creator of all things need to experiment on anyone physically, terrorize them, or make genetic changes?

The Scriptures must be our guide. One must read and read, until the very character of God is revealed by what is written there. After that anyone can see that what is being done by aliens goes against everything God stands for. THE ENEMY HAS DONE THIS.

Someday every knee shall bow above the Earth, on the Earth, and below the Earth. This Scripture indicates that God not only knows who they are, but where they are and tells us they have knees that can bow.

Betty Hill, one of the first reported abductees, drew a map and later found it corresponded to the star system of Reticulum. Another person was told that they (the aliens who looked similar to humans) were from a planet in our own solar system, but we never see them because they are always hidden behind a planet that we do observe. Astronauts have made claims to have seen bases of UFOs on the Moon and have been followed by them on various space missions. The general impression is that they do not want us in space.

So many things have gone wrong on space missions with The Challenger being the most tragic. One might wonder if sabotage was involved. Not by humans, but by creatures from elsewhere, who are determined to keep us out of space.

This subject was a real struggle for me and I didn't want to believe it, so it has taken me awhile to obey what God has told me to do. Aliens are not from other planets and have not been visiting us. They are 'all' inter-dimensional. I have just become really aware of the possibilities presented by cloning. Fallen angels (who are bound in the heaven-lies) may no longer mate with human women, but have been cloning humans and using organic robots that are occupied by earth bound demons. Demons are the spirit remains of the first civilization on Earth ruled by Lucifer. They seek embodiment and will possess, obsess, and influence humans in any way that's open to them. Using an or-ganic robot or cloned being gives them the ad-vantage of not having to contend with the will of a host. I believe this is what was left be-hind in the Roswell crash and perhaps other crashes.

This was a hard thing for me to deal with. I have always wanted to think others could visit us and space was the new frontier. There still might be life 'out there', but if it is, I think Earth is the forbidden planet to them un-til man is ready and the Earth and its inhabi-tants have gone through its' final judgment. We who belong to God, will then rule and reign over the Earth and the rest of the universe with Him. Then we'll get to meet the 'others' if they are any out there.

Chapter 10:

The Alien Agenda

The alien agenda seems apparent after studying the experiences of several abductees. In John Mack's book, ABDUCTION: HUMAN ENCOUNTERS WITH ALIENS. One such abductee, whose name remains confidential, says in essence.:

The first step is the creation of the children. Egg and sperm combined with aliens create these hybrids. Afterward an Earth parent is paired with an alien parent. The two create a bond between them so the offspring can be raised as both alien and human. After the Earth has been depopulated these Earth parents and alien parents intend to repopulate the Earth with these human/alien hybrids."

This abductee claims to be a hybrid himself.

While he was in the alien ship, he claims he was shown pictures of nuclear explosions, sections of Europe and the United States destroyed, a lot of people burned, a lot of people in terror, and the human race changing its form and texture.

There has been a battle going on between beings from all over the universe who is going to get control of the Earth. He was given the impression that this battle for control has been going on for thousand years and was shown as all coming to a head.

Prophecy, revelations, and people being taken up in what Christian religion calls "the rapture" were mentioned. According to these aliens such a removal has nothing to do with religion, for there are ships in place for that to happen.

This self declared human/alien abductee, objected to the word "rapture" and preferred instead to speak of the beings coming to help us to the next place of evolution. The slate is going to be wiped clean. It will be a whole new millennium of the Earth that will be supporting a whole "other" world. There is a bargaining going on among greater forces that are actually renegotiating the future of the planet. He again sees people ascending during a period of time when many terrible things are happening on the Earth.

This abductee's role will be to help the alien female make babies, take care of them, and become a leader of a new, original tribe, and new race of humans. According to him, the Earth's population will be destroyed in the blink of an eye and nothing can be done to prevent it. The hybrid humans would come down from the ships in sections to repopulate the Earth. These hybrids would have the knowledge from another world and would be prepared to start a new life. A whole system would be transplanted.

One can see from this that these aliens know how to appeal to the human ego. This abductee sees himself as a new Adam. He believes the whole human race will be dependent on him and his alien cohorts for existence.

As for the fate of the original humans according to this, there will be many left, but plagues, pestilence, and other disasters would destroy the structure of civilization. The entire society would crumble.

The aliens have caused this abductee to believe that this will usher in a new golden age of learning, openness, and opportunity. People of this abductees's age (in his twenties in 1993) were the first generation in this process. Their hybrid children are the second generation.

He has a sense that the aliens are connected with God, whatever that god is. As intermediaries, they are doing the same things that humans would do if they came across a species of anything that was on the brink of extinction. The humans would try to help them without direct intervention. The beings were acting (with God) to breed for the highest qualities of mankind.

One can see the horrible deception. The rapture (or catching away) of the church is being credited to alien beings, and they are put on the same level as gods. Here is an example of the wheat and the tares. The seed is even now being sown by the enemy.

As stated in this book earlier, God intends that a pure Adamite race rule planet Earth. God has never needed any help in creating a race of beings. Where were these aliens when He created the universe?

The wheat and the tares will grow together for awhile, perhaps through the Millennium; then the tares will be separated out and burned. God is still in control!

The fallen angels still influence and leave technology in places for man to find and trip over. Cloning is one of those technologies. Demons must have a physical body to operate through. Clones and organic robots would be the perfect answer. Demons could have complete control without contending with the will of a host. Fallen angels must remain in the heavenlies, but they can help the demons do their thing by providing them with the bodies they need to complete the plan to overthrow and destroy man, God's most precious creation.

I am a Star Trek fan and love the idea of traveling through space and meeting different peoples 'out there.' This was so hard for me to accept. I can't begin to tell you, but think about it. If you look up descriptions of demons and what they do and the effect they have you can't help but see the similarity between them and how people describe aliens.

They maybe others out there somewhere, but if there is they are forbidden to visit us until the final war between good and evil has been completed here.

All is not lost. Someday those who have chosen to make Jesus Christ their Savior and Lord will be heirs together with Him to rule and reign over the earth and the universe one day.

Chapter 11:

Ezekiel's Wheels

The flying saucers of describe cherubim, angelic creatures that move God's throne from place to place, as stated. To make them flying saucers or anything else is entirely out of harmony with Scripture. Some of the similarities between angelic beings and UFOs could exist because they were originally taught by angels; fallen angels. The following are some of the similarities and differences between UFOs and Ezekiel's wheels:

- Flashing cloud and glowing amber metal - Same
- Four living creatures, four different faces, four wings - Different
- Likeness of a man, not always straight legs, sole of foot like a calf's foot - Similar
- Sparkled like burnished bronze (glow) - Same
- Hands of a man on their four sides under their wings - Totally Different
- Their wings touched one another different they all went straight forward together - Similar
- Face of a man in front, face of a lion on the right side an ox on the left side, and an eagle in the back - Different
- In the midst of the living creatures were burning coals of fire like torches moving to and fro among them; the fire was bright and out of the fire went lightning - Similar to aliens balls of light
- Living creatures darted back and forth like a flash of lightning. Similar
- Man-size wheel on the ground gleamed like chrysolyte and their construction was a wheel within a wheel - Same

- Went in one of four directions without turning – Different, UFOs dart and turn
- Rims full of eyes - Similar if eyes are windows
- When the living creatures went, the wheels went beside them, and when the creatures went, the wheels went beside them, and when the living creatures were lifted up, the wheels were lifted up – Different, aliens are inside their craft, not on the outside
- Wherever the spirit went, the creatures went, and the wheels rose along with them, for the spirit of life of the four living creatures was in the wheels - Different
- Over the head of the living creatures there was a likeness of a firmament, looking terrible and awesome. It had crystal or ice stretched across the expanse of sky over their heads – Different
- Under the firmament their wings were stretched out straight, one toward another. Every living creature had two wings, which covered its body on one side and two on the other side. When they went, the sound of their wings was like the noise of great water - Different
- There was a voice above the firmament that was over their heads. When they stood they let down their wings - Different
- And above the firmament that was over their heads was the likeness of a throne, in appearance like a sapphire stone; and seated above the likeness of the throne was a likeness with the appearance of a MAN! - Different THIS WAS THE GLORY OF THE LORD!

Chapter 12:

Man's Dominion

In Scripture, whatever is said about angels, demons, pre-Adamites, and other creatures not of the present race and creation on Earth is limited to that which is necessary to reveal God's plan for man.

In 1 Timothy 5:21, we read of elect angels; and the term is no doubt used in the same sense as of elect men who are redeemed. We then conclude that angels did have some means of grace and reconciliation, and that some are called elect because they became reconciled.

God, who is all good, has always given mercy to rebels of the human race, but the bible does not tell us He was just as merciful to angels, demons, and pre-Adamite rebels, providing them with a means of grace befitting their nature and creative purposes.

Lucifer was the first to be exalted in pride; and he and his angelic followers were the first to attempt the overthrow of God's government. They were responsible for Earth's first sinful career. Had they remained true to God, there would have been no Flood and chaos as described in Genesis 1:2; and therefore, no need of the six days of Genesis 1:3-2:25 to restore the Earth to a second habitable state, and no need for the creation of new land animals, fish, fowls, and man to rule the planet Earth. Lucifer and the pre-Adamites would have continued to live on the Earth and carry out the dominion over the Earth now designed for man.

The entire Bible message is centered on the complete redemption of man, which includes ridding the Earth of all rebellion. This includes all alien occupants of UFOs and any of their human/alien offspring. This is so that the new heavens and new earth and the original state of the universal kingdom of God will be fully restored and God will be in all eternally. (1 Corinthians 15:24-28; Ephesians 1:10; and Revelation 21 and 22).

When Adam rebelled, the Earth entered its second sinful career. In God's plan, we are now nearing the end of Adam's rebellion. In Ephesians 1:11, it says, *"Moreover, because of what Christ has done we have become gifts to God that He delights in, for as part of God's sovereign plan we were chosen from the beginning to be His, and all things happen just as He decided long ago."*

In Psalms 8:4-6, it says, *"What is man that you are mindful of him and the son of (earth born) man that You care for him? Yet you have made him but a little lower than God (or heavenly beings) and You have crowned him with glory and honor. You made him to have dominion over the works of your hands; You have put all things under his feet"* (Amplified Bible) See also Hebrews 1:6-10

The inhabitants of the Earth must be judged for sin. This is why the seven seal judgments, the seven trumpet judgments, the seven vial judgments must occur during the seven years of Tribulation soon to come. God specifies how many will be killed in each instance and promises that there will be a physical remnant from every nation left alive to go into the Millennium. If human/alien hybrids are included, it can only be as in the parable of the wheat and the tares. They will be left to grow together, and at the end of the thousand years, they will be weeded out and burned along with other rebels against God.

God is soon to send Jesus Christ with the armies of Heaven to defeat the armies of Antichrist and seize control of the Earth. This He will do in one day (Zechariah 4:7)! This will be for the express purpose of putting down all rebellion, so as to restore God's sovereignty in all parts of the universe, as obtained before Lucifer and Adam rebelled. Whether these hybrids will be allowed to live through the Millennium depends on whether they obey God's government laws. Those who obey only because they have to and have no heart-felt allegiance to God will be weeded out at the end of the thousand years when Satan is loosed out of the abyss, where he has been imprisoned for the thousand years. He will lead away those who desire to rebel against God.

After this the armies of God and Satan will once again clash. This is when all rebellion will be put down once and for all. The Earth and the atmospheric heavens will be cleansed by fire. How will mankind survive this? See the chapter on "Fire."

Saints, the redeemed ones of the human race from the time of Adam to the second advent of Christ, will be the future kings and priests under God the Father and Christ to reign over the dominion originally given to Adam. (Psalms

8, Isaiah 9:6-7; Daniel 2:44-45; 7:13, 18, 27; Zechariah 4; Luke 1:32-33; Acts 15:13-18; 2 Thessalonians 1:7-10; Jude 14-15; Revelation 1:5; 5:10; 11:15; 20:4-6; 22:1-5)

The passage in Psalms 8 places man at the head of all God's works, the heavens, including the sun, moon, stars and the Earth, including all living things. It makes him next to God in position and power over all creation. This includes the alien occupants of any UFOs.

Thus Adam was originally made higher than the angels, but by sin he was brought very low and made subject to death. Now man is in his lessened state, short of God's glory (Romans 3:23), below angels. Christ Himself was made lower for a time to take man's low place and raise him again higher than angels, as he originally was. Christ has been exalted again to a place higher than angels or any other being except the Father. Redeemed man is to be raised up to that exalted position with Him. (Romans 8:17-18; Ephesians 2:6-7; 3:8-10; 2 Timothy 2:12; Hebrews 2:5-11: Revelation 1:5, 5:10; 22:4-6) By now all those who have accepted Christ as their Savior and are in the ranks of the redeemed should be shouting for joy!

The redeemed men and women who rule and reign with Christ will then have their glorified bodies. Israel will be ruled by the original, King David. The twelve tribes will be headed up by the twelve apostles. The King of Kings and Lord of Lords is Christ Himself.

Those left alive after the Tribulation will be able to live in their physical bodies forever.

They will procreate to fill the Earth once again with the race of man. More will be written on this in the chapter called, "Future World".

God must be recognized by all as the supreme moral governor of the universe. Until free moral agents of all kinds learn these lessons, they naturally are in ignorance of certain facts and need training.

One of the chief reasons for God's dealing with man was to bring him back to the place where he was before his fall. Having purged man of all possibility of falling in the future, God will place redeemed man in his original position of having dominion over all things.

Thus, God does not have the slightest doubt as to the future of His plan for man. If all men were to see and understand this clearly, no outside influence no matter from where it came, could persuade them that they were an inferior race.

Please take note that these aliens/demons are trying to merge with us. They want to share in our destiny. They want the planet that God has made for us! No wonder some of them seem malevolent. We will someday rule over them!

By creating hybrids that look like us, they hope to fool God into letting them be a part of the ruling class! Once again the parable of the wheat and the tares comes to mind. The fallen angels and the giants could not fool God and neither will these creatures.

<u>ALL FREE WILLS MUST EVENTUALLY LEARN:</u>
1) That God must be respected and obeyed.
2) That His laws are final and just.
3) That sin does not pay and will never be excused.
4) That God's form of government is the only correct one.
5) That a loving and free submission to God is the highest and most noble principle of free moral government.
6) That justice and righteousness must prevail, or no society can be eternally preserved in the universe.
7) That consecration to the greatest good of all is the nature and highest glory of the creature.
8) That God is merciful and forgiving to rebels who will be penitent and who learn obedience through their experiences.
9) That God is the only absolutely just and perfect Being, and the only one capable and worthy of unquestioned authority.
10) That all the accusations of the present rebels against God are untrue.
11) That God does only those things that are for the common good of all creation.

God's eternal plan for man and want he wants to bring to pass on earth is known from the beginning to the end and what He plans He has power to do. All who conform to His plan will receive the predestined blessings and those who willfully rebel will be cursed with the predestined punishments. It is left up to each person to choose his own destiny. God wants all men to be saved, but if man does not choose to be saved, that is his responsibility (2 Timothy 2:4; 2 Peter 3:9; John 3:16; Revelation 22:17).

Moses declared that man was made in the image and likeness of God. The Hebrew for image is 'tselem,' meaning model, shape, fashion, similitude, and BODILY resemblance, as proved in places where it is used. (Matthew 22:20; Acts 19:35; Romans 1:23; 8:29; 11:4; 1 Corinthians 15:49; 2 Corinthians 4:4; Colossians 1:15; Hebrews 10:1; Revelation 13:14-15; 14:9-11; 15:2; 16:2; 19:20; 20:4)

This sheds some light on why these aliens/demons are so determined to look like us. The apostle Paul said that man was *"the image and glory of God"* (1 Corinthians 11:7)

These aliens/demons have been in existence far longer than we have. Some are fallen angels and some are the demons spirits of the human/angel hybrids killed during Noah's flood.

God has given the revelation of Himself, His Creation, and His plan for man, so that man might know his origin, present responsibility, and destiny. The Bible is the record of this revelation. God appraises man as the highest of creation making him lord of creation (Genesis 1:26-31; Psalms 83:8). He has spent many millennia of effort to redeem him (Hebrews 1:1-3; 2 Peter 3:9) and even gave His only begotten Son to redeem man(John 3:16).

Gos has even promised to restore man to his original dominion as eternal ruler of creation (Daniel 7:18, 27: Revelation 5:10; 22:4-5) and entrusted man with the eternal authority and life to help God administer the affairs of the universe (Romans 8:17-18; Revelation 2:27-28; 5:10; 22:4-5).

Man has been placed on an equal basis with Jesus Christ in redemption and made joint heirs in inheritance (Romans 8:17), suffering and future glory (Matthew 10:24-25; Romans 8:18; 2 Timothy 2:13, 1 Peter 2:21; 4:1; Revelations 2:26-27; 5:10; 22:4-5). God has made provisions for body, soul, and spirit, here and hereafter.

Why do alien/demons cause people to turn from believing in God or cause confusion in man's beliefs? It is a delaying action, so we will not know who we really are!

Chapter 13

Fire!

At the end of the Millennium, when God defeats all of Satan's armies for the last time, with fire that cleanses the Earth and the atmospheric heaven, how is the race of man going to survive?

In Exodus 3:2-3, it says *"Then was Nebuchadnezzar filled with fury and his face was made dark with anger at Shadrach, Meshach, and Abednego, and threw them into the fire. So they bound them tight with ropes and cast them into the furnace, fully clothed. And because the king, in his anger, had demanded such a hot fire in the furnace, the flames leaped out, and killed the soldiers as they threw them in! So Shadrach, Meshach, and Abednego fell down bound into the roaring flames. But suddenly as he was watching Nebuchadnezzar jumped up in amazement and exclaimed to his advisors, "Didn't we throw three men into the furnace?" Yes," they said, "We did indeed, Your Majesty." "Well, Look!" Nebuchadnezzar shouted. "I see four men, unbound, walking around in the fire, and they aren't even hurt by the flames! And the fourth looks like a god!"Then Nebuchadnezzar came as close as he could to the open door of the flaming furnace and yelled, "Shadrach, Meshach, and Abednego, servants of the Most High God! Come out! Come Here" So they stepped out of the fire. Then the princes, governors, captains and counselors crowded around them and saw that the fire hadn't touched them. Not a hair of their heads was singed; their coats were not scorched and they didn't even smell of smoke! Then Nebuchadnezzar said, "Blessed be the God of Shad-*

rach, Meshach, and Abednego, for he sent his angel to deliver his trusting servants when they defied the king's commandment and were willing to die rather than serve or worship any god except their own."

The same God who spoke from the burning bush and protected the three Hebrew children from the flames will protect those who belong to Him when the Earth and atmospheric heavens are burned. If mankind can make "smart bombs," then God can surely make "smart fire!"

The clothes of the three Hebrew children did not even smell like fire, nor was their hair so much as even singed, and yet those who threw them in were killed instantly. God has command of fire and can do with it as He pleases. When Elijah was mocking the prophets of Baal, God sent fire that licked up thousands of gallons of water. There is that "smart" fire again!

The fire that changes the heavens and the earth and destroys all the evil rebels at the end of the Millennium will only destroy that which is evil, even disease germs and other unwanted pests, including demons and whatever aliens are still lurking in our atmospheric heavens at the time.

At that time all the oceans will be evaporated and water will be supplied through rivers, lakes, underground springs, and streams. Think of the massive amounts of land that will be uncovered for man to explore and live on!

The Earth will never be destroyed, only renovated. The Earth is eternal and, as it says in

Psalms 104:5, *"that it should not be removed forever."*

In 2 Peter 3:10-13, it says, *"But the day of the Lord will come as a thief in the night in the which the heavens shall pass away with a great noise and the elements shall melt with the fervent heat; the earth also and the works that are therein shall be burned up. Seeing then that all these things shall be dissolved, what manner of persons ought ye to be in all holy conversation (behavior) and godliness. Looking for and hasting unto the coming of the day of the Lord, wherein the heavens being on fire shall be dissolved, and the elements shall melt with fervent heat? Nevertheless we, according to His promise, Look for new heavens and a new earth wherein dwelleth righteousness."*

TERMINOLOGY
Pass away: Comes from the Greek parerchomai, pass from one condition to another, It never means annihilation.

Elements: Refers to the principles of basic elements of the present world system of evil spirits, disease, germs, corruption, and all elements by which men corrupt themselves.
Melt: Means the losing of the atmospheric heavens and the Earth from the curse by fire, not their annihilation.
Works: Works, toil, deeds, labor, and acts of men (houses, structures, etc.) This will include religious works as well.
Burned up: Burn down to the ground, wholly consume with fire. It has reference to the things of the earth and man that need to be removed,

so that the things that need not be moved may remain eternally. (Hebrews 12:25-28)

Seeing then: That all the things of Earth and of man that need to be removed will be burned up, leaving only those things that need not to be burned to remain; let us live godly and holy lives.

Looking For: Let us look forward to the renewal of the earth and to the day of God in the new Earth when He will be all in all as before rebellion and sin (1 Corinthians 15:24-28; Revelation 21:1-22:5).

Promise: See Isaiah 65:17 and 66:22-24. The Earth will have been made new three times:
1) At its first creation;
2) At the recreation in the six days of Genesis 1:3 to 2:25;
3) At the renovation of the heavens and the earth by fire (Revelation 21).

The Earth was originally created to be inhabited (Isaiah 45:18) This purpose will be realized forever when the natural people who do not rebel with Satan at the end of the Millennium (Revelation 20:7-10) will remain on the Earth after its renovation by fire and multiply forever, as God intended Adam and his race to do before the Fall.

The following Scriptures are included to prove God intends that man be on Earth forever:

- *"An God said, "This is the token of the covenant which I make between me and you and every living creature that is with you, for PERPETUAL GENERATIONS."* (Genesis 9:12)

- *"The secret things belong unto the Lord our God, but those things which are revealed belong unto us and to our children FOREVER, that we may do all the words of the law."* (Deuteronomy 29:29)

- *"He shall be great, and shall be called the Son of the Highest, the throne of his father David. And he shall reign over the house of Jacob FOREVER; and of his kingdom there shall be no end."* (Luke 1:32-33)

- *"And hath made us kings and priests unto God and his father; to Him be glory and dominion forever and ever. Amen."* (Revelation 1:6)

- *"And hast made us unto our God kings and priests, and we shall reign on the earth."* (Revelation 5:10)

- *"And if children, then heirs, heirs of God, and joint heirs with Christ; if so be that we suffer with him, that we may be also glorified together."* (Romans 8:17)

- *"Do ye not know that the saints shall judge the world? And if the world shall be judged by you, are ye unworthy to judge the smallest matters? Know ye not that ye shall judge angels? How much more the things that pertain to this life?"* (1 Corinthians 6:2-3)

- *"Of the increase of His government and peace there shall be NO END, upon the throne of David, and upon his kingdom, to order it, and to establish it with judgment and with justice from henceforth even FOREVER."* (Isaiah 9:7)

- *"But the saints of the most High shall take the kingdom and possess the kingdom FOREVER, EVEN FOREVER AND EVER."* (Daniel 7:18)

- *"And the kingdom and dominion, and the greatness of the kingdom under the whole heaven, shall be given to the people of the saints of the most High, whose kingdom is an EVERLASTING KINGDOM, and all dominions shall* serve and obey him."(Daniel 7:27)

- *"And ye shall keep it a feast unto the Lord seven days in the year. It shall be a statute FOREVER in your generations; ye shall celebrate it in the seventh month."* (Leviticus 23:42)

- *"One ordinance shall be both for you of the congregation, and also for the stranger that sojourneth with, an ordinance FOREVER in your generations; as ye are, so shall the stranger be before the Lord."* (Numbers 15:15)

Chapter 14:
Will The World End?

The aliens that pilot the various crafts known as UFOs have predicted massive earthquakes, tidal waves, wars, pestilence, and disease. As a result of all this, they say, the Earth will be depopulated and they intend to be the ones to repopulate it. All this is to come about because of the careless and destructive way that we treat planet Earth.

God's Word has forewarned of these days of destruction. There are to be seven years of Tribulation, also known as Jacob's Trouble. God will pour out His wrath upon the Earth as He once did upon Sodom and Gomorrah and for the same reason. These disasters of nature are god's judgment on sin. Man is to be judged for his behavior toward God and his fellow-man, not because of how he has treated the planet.

In Leviticus, 18:21-30, it says, *"And thou shalt not let any of thy seed pass through the fire to Molech, neither shalt thou profane the name of God; I am the Lord. Thou shalt not lie with mankind, as with womankind; it abomination. Neither shalt thou like with any beast to defile thyself therewith; neither shall any woman stand before a beast to lie down thereto it is confusion. Defile ye not yourselves in any of these things;* (See verses 1-20 of the same chapter to know what the rest of these 'things' are) *for in all these the nations are defiled which I cast out before you; and the land is defiled; therefore I do visit the iniquity thereof upon it, and the LAND ITSELF VOMITEST OUT HER INHABITANTS. Ye shall therefore* keep my statutes and my judgments, and shall not commit any of these abominations; neither any of your own nation, nor any stranger that sojourneth among you. For all these abominations have the men of the land done, which were before you, and the land is defiled. That the land SPUE NOT YOU OUT ALSO, when ye defile it, as it spued out the nations that were before you. For whosoever shall commit any of these abominations, even the souls that commit them shall be cut off from among their people. Therefore shall ye keep mine ordinance, that ye commit not any one of these abominable customs, which were committed before you, and that ye defile not yourselves therein: I am the Lord you God."

Some of the things listed in previous verses are adultery, fornication, and incest. These sins are prevalent in society today and are glossed over as "doing your own thing", but there is a price to pay.

How would one list the willing sexual encounter with aliens? Would it be lying with beasts, fornication, adultery, or a combination of all three? One can be sure it is certainly not inspired by God, for it goes against His own Word. Those victimized against their will are the same as victims of rape and abduction. Their attackers will be held responsible.

The blood of millions of innocent babies that were never born, but were slaughtered in their mother's wombs cries out to God for justice. Instead of being sacrificed to the god, Molech, they have been sacrificed to the god of convenience.

Earthquakes could be described as the land vomiting out its inhabitants. There will be several earthquakes, with the final one affecting the whole planet and being described as leveling mountains, shifting continents, and causing islands to disappear.

The Earth will be hit by a meteor that will land in the sea, and a third of all things, including men, in the sea will be destroyed. There is also to be hail and fire mixed with blood that will burn up a third of the earth and all the green grass.

A comet will hit rivers of water that will cause the water to become poison and kill many people and animals. Horrible demons from the abyss will be loosed to torture and kill another third of mankind. Wars, disease, and starvation will also take a massive toll.

We have been warned for thousands of years that these things will come to pass. These aliens insist it is our behavior toward the planet that causes these horrors to happen. God states it is man's behavior toward him and toward his neighbor that causes it. Who are you going to believe?

Even if every person in the world became an ecology advocate and environmentalist, it would be impossible to stop tidal waves, earthquakes, and meteors by saving the whales, spotted owls, plant life, or the ozone layer.

God does have a plan of escape, in 2 Chronicles 7:14 it says:

If my people, which are called by my name, shall humble themselves, and pray, and seek my face, and turn from their wicked ways; then will I hear from Heaven, and will forgive their sin, and will HEAL THEIR LAND."

It is not too likely that all men in all lands will do what this verse says, but the ones who do will be spared as individuals and as nations.

Besides judging evil men, these events have another purpose as well. In Psalms 26:9, it says:

"for when thy judgments are in the earth, the inhabitants of the world (universe) will learn righteousness."

As stated in other sections of this book, there will be a remnant of humans (not aliens) from most of the nations of the Earth to live on into the Millennium and beyond. God's plans for the race of man go on forever. The aliens cannot change that!

So many times throughout Scripture, God has referred to us as sheep. Anyone who has ever been around sheep has to be aware that they are some of the most stupid and totally defenseless animals that there are. They are preyed upon by many vicious and powerful predators. Their only defense is the shepherd.

"All we like sheep have gone astray." It sounds like we have no more sense than sheep. This is not an insult, but it is to show that our only power and defense is a dependence on the obedience to the Great Shepherd, Jesus Christ.

To illustrate the truth of this, let us review some of the predators lurking about to destroy us:

1) Satan himself, who is the mastermind behind all our predators;
2) Fallen angels, who rule nations and leaders to our detriment as well as commanding Earth's population of demons;
3) Demons, who seek to disrupt all men by disease, confusion, insanity, and disharmony. They cannot directly affect us physically unless we succumb to them and allow them to do so. They can possess a human or an animal. Angels and aliens cannot;
4) Aliens from all origins are Satan's high-tech terrorists; apparently no more fallen angels are willing to spend their eternity chained in a cavern of darkness in the Earth, so these aliens have been recruited to do basically some of the same things the fallen angels once did by contaminating the race of man.

What do terrorists do? They torture, infiltrate, terrorize, rape, kill, and appeal to a person's pride by convincing their "victims" to sympathize with their cause and some of them end up willingly sleeping with the enemy.

Those who continue to resist are made to feel helpless, and insignificant. These aliens are every bit as dangerous as evil angels, in that they are able to make themselves a part of our society without being "noticed." They become wolves in sheep's clothing.

Satan knows his time is short, and he is using all his resources to destroy the race of man because he hates God and is bitterly jealous of God's most beloved creation, man. Even though he knows what his eventual future is, he is determined to take as many of the sons of Adam with him as he can.

Could these aliens be God's creation, too. If so it would seem He wanted them to learn by what they observe here and repent of their rebellion, as well, instead of trying to become a part of God's plan by physically merging with us. They have to see that the change He wants is a spiritual one, not a physical one.

They have a spiritual darkness in them or they would be following God's plan and not Satan's. They do not seem to realize that they, too, are being used and that their "boss'" will discard them as quickly as anyone else, when they fail in their goal. It does not pay to follow a loser!

In the perilous days ahead, as the predators around us become more vicious, cunning, and numerous, we "sheep" must learn to stay ever closer to our only defense, The Shepherd!

We must rely on the weapons He supplies. Satan himself and his fallen angels and the demons must obey the word when spoken with authority. By using the name of JESUS, those of us who belong to Him can bind Satan and command demons to leave their victims.

The same God also has power over aliens. By using the name of Jesus, we can also command them to let us alone. God has a duty to protect His children when they call on Him for help. The job of the Shepherd is to provide for the needs of the sheep, shelter the sheep, and PROTECT His sheep.

Without Him we can do nothing!

Chapter 15:

Surrounded by Enemies

By the time the smoke clears and the Earth stops shaking, what kind of world will be left? Some of the geological changes indicated in Scripture is very descriptive of the changes in the Middle East. One is that the Dead Sea which is now the lowest place on the Earth will be raised up and have inlet and outlet rivers of water. There will be one road that leads to Jerusalem. The Mount of Olives will be divided into two parts. Jerusalem itself will be divided. Egypt will become a wasteland for forty years as one of the judgments for its history of persecuting the Jews.

Many experts have predicted that the west coast of the United States, especially California, is due for a huge earthquake that will probably cause all or most of the western coastline to disappear beneath the sea. The eastern seaboard could also suffer the same fate. The United States will probably become two continents with dividing lines at the Mississippi River from the Gulf of Mexico through Canada.

At the end of the Battle of Armageddon, the nations of the world will be judged according to how they have treated the nation of Israel all through the centuries. Any student of history will know which nations have the most to fear at this judgment. Those individuals of these nations who refuse to repent will be eaten up of a disease that causes the skin to melt off their bones and their eyeballs to melt out of their sockets.

It will take the nation of Israel months and years to clean up the mess left from that last horrible battle. A whole new army of workers who will do nothing but bury the dead and clean up the debris will be kept busy for years.

The government of the Millennium will be a theocracy which means "ruled by God" with Jesus as King of kings and Lord of lords. A resurrected and glorified King David will rule over all of Israel. The apostles will rule over one tribe each.

All saints from the time of Adam to the Tribulation will be judged and rewarded according to the deeds done in the body and will be given places of ruler-ship according to the degree of their rewards.

The seat of government will be a restored and rebuilt Jerusalem which will be the world capital and center of worship forever. It will be worldwide and will forever increase in population and blessings.

Some men of all nations now in existence on the Earth will continue as natural people in the kingdom forever and ever. *"All people, nations, and languages should serve Him, His dominion is an everlasting dominion, which shall not pass away, and Hid Kingdom that which shall not be destroyed."* (Daniel 7:13, 14, 18, 22-27; Isaiah 9:6-7; Zechariah 14:1-12; Luke 1:32-35 and Revelation 11:15)

In that future world every nation will enjoy a state of universal peace. There will be no tempter since Satan will be bound for the dura-

tion of the Millennium. There will be no taxa-
tion to keep up armies and navies.

Class prejudices will be forgotten because of
the great turning to God by all nations after
hearing the gospel. Spiritual revival will
break out in every land and all people will become one in serving the Great King.

There will be universal property, no corrupt
politicians, and full justice for all. Crime
waves will be things of the past. The Lord and
His glorified saints will try men and also
judge them, thus assuring justice to all alike.
Justice will be perfect and swift. No slick
lawyers will be able to get criminals off on a
technicality again.

In that future world, every nation will be required to go once a year to the Feast of Taber-
nacles in Jerusalem If they do not, God will
hold the rain and cause their crops to fail.
There will be trees of life lining the streets
there for the healing of the nations and individuals. No one need ever be sick or infirm
again.

The nature of animals will be changed. All will
be vegetarians. Man will be able to have any
animal as a pet in perfect safety. The enmity
between man and animals will be gone.

Human life will be prolonged (Isaiah 65:20;
Zechariah 8:4; Luke 1:33) Life will be prolonged to a thousand years and then those who
do not join Satan in rebellion at the end of
the Millennium will be permitted to live forever. Men will continue to live in linear time,

not inter-dimensional. We are promised there will be days and seasons forever.

The Millennium will give men all over the world the opportunity to know Jesus and His plan of salvation. The Jews will be the evangelists of that day.

There will be no aliens allowed to live on the Earth. They will be separated from among us as the giants once were. At the end of the Millennium when Satan is loosed again for a short time to gather another army of rebels, God will make swift end of anyone who choose to rebel by destroying them with fire. This will include any alien, demon, evil angel, disease germ, or any kind of evil or corruption. Thus the Earth will finally be cleansed and made perfect.

Those believers from the beginning of the creation of man to the time of the rapture will be in their glorified bodies.

These bodies will be like the body of Jesus. Jesus could walk through walls and appear and disappear at will. He could eat and drink as well. All believers will have the same ability.

Anyone who has ever watched Star Trek the Next Generation and has seen an episode with "Q" from the "Q" continuum can get an idea of some of the abilities the saints of God will have without "Q"'s bad attitude.

After the Millennium innumerable people will have been redeemed and glorified as immortal beings to help God administer the affairs of the universe and rule all coming generations.

Man will no longer be placed on probation to see if he will obey God, for he will have gone through all the testing necessary and will have proved himself true to God. At this time Earth's governments will continue to be governed by the redeemed and it will be a success forever. There will be no more failure, for the redeemed and natural man will have been purged of any possibility of failure.

By this time Earth will be rid of Satan, fallen angels, demons, and any aliens that have done their part to hurt the race of man.

God has been merciful beyond measure. The race of man has been plagued by so many outside influences to turn him from God that perhaps this is one of the reasons God has chosen us to rule. Those who overcome these other voices and influences and still choose to follow God in spite of all have won God's special heart of mercy.

The new heaven and new earth are the result of the renovation of 2 Peter 3:10-13. There will be new lands. See Revelation 21:1 which says, *"And I saw a new heaven and a new earth; for the first heaven and the first earth were passed away; and there was no more sea."*

The large oceans covering about three fourths of the Earth will be no more, having been evaporated by the fervent heat when the Earth is renovated. The planet Earth will be green and watered by rains, rivers, lakes and streams. We will have all of eternity to explore its wonders. This will be a vast area when the great oceans are gone. There will be an abundance of rivers, lakes and small seas on the Earth forever (Psalms 72:8-10, 17; 97:1-6; Isaiah 42:4, 10:12, 66:19-21; Zechariah 9:10; Ezekiel 47:1-23)

Some seas were originally created with the Earth to be eternal and will last as long as Israel, the sun, moon and the Earth itself. (Jeremiah 5:22, 31:35, 36; Psalms 146:6; Proverbs 8:29; Acts 4:24; 14:15; Revelations 14:7) An abundance of water on the Earth will be necessary to fulfill prophecies speaking of fruitful seasons and waters springing up in the desert. (Genesis 8:22; Isaiah 35; Amos 5:8; 9:6; Job 38:4-16, 22:30; Psalms 104:5-14, 24-28)

Someday when man has allowed God to open his mind and give him the wisdom to do so, man will reach out successfully to the stars. That will be the final frontier "To finally go where no man has gone before!" The saints and faithful angels will share in supervising those who go out into the vastness of space. None of these present intruders will be allowed to stop us. At that time will be able to meet some of those "other sheep" who are out there somewhere.

Meanwhile it would be good to start all our prayers as the Jews do to remind us of who we are and most importantly of who He is.

BLESSED ART THOU O LORD OUR GOD: KING OF THE UNIVERSE!

Conclusion

Why don't they just kill us? Earth, the most sought after piece of real estate in the universe, is up for grabs. Or is it? Surely the aliens have acquired enough sperm, egg, and other tissue samples by this time, so why not just kill us and take over?

Simple, the last battle of this present age will be a spiritual one, not technological. If superior technology were all that is required, we would be long gone.

Many scientists and those in the intelligence business believe that superior technology is what wins the game and have collaborated with the enemy to elevate our technology. Our own culture seems to bear out his theory of better gadgets, more superiority.

The aliens have figured this out about us and have us "toys" to play with as a diversion, much in the same way we would divert a rambunctious two-year-old who is trying to destroy mother's favorite vase. Give the child a bright-colored toy that hums, clicks and moves, and he will soon forget the vase.

Those in the intelligence game have probably been given just enough "toys' to divert them from what empowers the human race to become the superior race, which is faith in Almighty God.

Were we all to die suddenly, as the dinosaurs once did, it would only serve to release the faithful to their final stage of redemption, which is receiving their glorified bodies that live forever and have the same power that Christ had after his resurrection. No technology needed!!

The ruling class would then be established once and for all; end of story as far as these aliens' aspirations are concerned.

Imagine being able to travel anywhere at the speed of a thought, being able to appear or disappear, walk through walls. This new body will look like the one we have now, only better. We will still be able to eat, feel, and do all the things we do now and so much more. Read the Scriptures that pertain to the things that Christ did after He was resurrected. He walked, talked, and ate with his disciples. They would touch Him and He was solid and yet he could disappear at will. Then we shall know "all things". The things we only dare to imagine and beyond our imaginings will become clear to us. Is it any wonder these aliens resent, fear, and hate us?

They want us alive, but deceived. Dead bodies are no good to them. They are out to divert mankind to the destruction of his spirit, not his body. They will do their best to lead us to believe in four great lies:
1) They are benevolent and are here to help us.
2) They seeded the Earth in the distant past, and we are the result.
3) Man's strength is within himself. He does not need God. They can help us reach this ultimate strength.
4) Only by cooperating with them can we survive, etc.

The end goal is the same as that of Satan and his angels. These aliens believe that once we have destroyed ourselves, or, I should say, have sold out our spiritual values for technology and power, they will be on hand to take over.

Satan is not about to share the lime-light with anyone. The deception set up by these aliens will be overturned by the Antichrist three and a half years into the seven year Tribulation period. Satan started planting the seeds of this ultimate deception a long, long time ago. The man who will call himself Christ and set himself up as a god will probably look very much like the face on the Shroud of Turin.

To kill us then is no answer. Deception is the most powerful tool that can be used to defeat us. *"For there shall arise false Christs, and false prophets, and shall show great signs and wonders; in so much that, if it were possible, they shall deceive the very elect."* Matthew 24:24. The only way to avoid being deceived is to know and study what God says.

CONCENTRATE ON SPIRITUAL VALUES. DO NOT BE DECEIVED BY THE TOYS AND TOOLS OF DESTRUCTION.